Leading the Curriculum in the Primary School

Leading the Curriculum in the Primary School

Neil Burton and Mark Brundrett

Paul Chapman Publishing

© Neil Burton and Mark Brundrett 2005

First published 2005

Paul Chapman Publishing
A SAGE Publications Company
1 Oliver's Yard
55 City Road
London EC1Y 1SP

SAGE Publications Inc
2455 Teller Road
Thousand Oaks, California 91320

SAGE Publications India Pvt Ltd
B-42 Panchsheel Enclave
Post Box 4109
New Delhi 110 017

Library of Congress Control Number: 2005925813

A catalogue record for this book is available from the British Library

ISBN 1-4129-0252-5
ISBN 1-4129-0253-3 (pbk)

Typeset by Pantek Arts Ltd, Maidstone, Kent
Printed on paper from sustainable resources
Printed in Great Britain by Athenaeum Press Ltd, Gateshead

Contents

For Pat Brundrett and Martine Burton

Preface

The concept of 'leadership' has overtaken previous linguistic formulations such as 'administration' or 'management' as the dominant description for all those functions that are involved in guiding and developing organizations towards the achievement of their organizational goals. This is not merely part of some general linguistic drift; it is a recognition that organizations and institutions, including schools, need to be constantly reinvigorated, monitored (in the broadest and best sense) and moved forward if they are to meet the needs of a rapidly changing world. The sheer pace of innovation in learning theory, in the use of ICT and above all in national policy on education has been so dramatic that it has, at times quite literally, taken the breath away from those engaged in learning and teaching in schools.

It is partly because of the amplitude of this wave of multiple and multi-layered innovations that some have argued for a new conception of leadership that moves away from traditional hierarchical models where power and responsibility are vested in one or two key people – namely, the headteacher and the deputy headteacher or, in larger schools, a slightly wider 'senior management team'. The central thesis of those who offer this new conception is that there is simply so much leadership and so many things to lead that all staff need to be involved as leaders. These new ideas come in various guises but one of the most popular and influential ways of expressing this trend is through the notion of 'distributed leadership', where leadership functions are spread widely throughout the school. In many ways this is to be applauded as an approach since it has the advantages of not only involving staff in decision-making but also of offering a degree of democratization (or something akin to it) in the leadership and management of schools.

There are, however, a number of challenges and dangers subsumed within these new ideas and these have especial impact on primary schools. These issues can be outlined in a series of questions:

- How will staff find time to take on new leadership responsibilities when it is almost inevitable in many primary schools that all teaching staff, possibly even including the headteacher, will have a full-time teaching commitment and a responsibility to a class of children?
- How can teachers who have received no specific training to be leaders take on complex and challenging roles in middle leadership which involve motivating and managing colleagues?
- Where will such aspirant middle leaders gain experience of key skills and competencies associated with developing and enacting strategic initiatives?

To some extent the answer to all these questions will be the same as it has always been: teachers will learn from one another and draw on their own, apparently infinite, resources of intelligence and creativity in order to make their schools meet the needs of children. These methods of experiential learning are not to be derided or underestimated as a strategy but they are not the only methods, nor necessarily the best methods, of learning how to be a leader in schools. For this reason this text sets out, quite self-consciously, to address these issues by attempting to provide some of the theoretical and practical underpinnings of this new conception of leadership.

The structure of the text is conceived in four sections that take the reader through the following areas: an overview of the issues associated with middle leadership; a detailed discussion of leadership and the emergent notion of the role of the middle leader in managing and accounting for change in schools; the resource issues that a middle leader may justifiably be expected to address; and, finally, the ways in which staff can be led by middle leaders. The final section concludes with a chapter on school-based research and evaluation for evidence-based practice.

Section A provides an overview of the components of middle leadership in primary schools. Chapter 1 serves as an introduction to the text and its title – 'In search of subject leadership' – reveals the fact that we still seek to define the role of middle leaders in Key Stages 1 and 2. Chapter 2 reflects on the effective classroom practitioner and Chapter 3 attempts to show how the skills built up in the classroom can be extrapolated and developed as teachers take on such middle leadership roles and move from subject to curriculum leadership. Section B guides the middle leader in establishing the direction of his or her subject area or department and commences with Chapter 4, which offers a more expansive and detailed analysis of what is actually meant by the terms leadership and management and then goes on to explore the role of the middle leader within the distributed leadership structure of a primary school. Chapter 5 provides a theoretical overview on middle leaders managing change and some detailed guidance relating to contemporary notions of strategic planning and target-setting. Chapter 6 offers guidance on monitoring and evaluating progress, and Chapter 7 discusses issues of accountability and the middle leader, especially as they relate to the Ofsted model of external inspection. Section C is devoted to resource issues, within which Chapter 8 concentrates on identifying and organizing learning resources and Chapter 9 adumbrates the problems and possibilities associated with a topic that is often new and challenging to middle leaders – that of budgeting for the cost of learning resources. The final element of the text, Section D, focuses on what the writers consider to be a key issue in enhancing schools, that of leading and motivating colleagues and pupils. Chapter 10 outlines the way in which colleagues need to be lead and managed to improve performance. Chapter 11 focuses on the various models of curriculum leadership and suggests that a co-constructed model of teaching and learning should be adopted which can both motivate pupils to learn and mirror the overall methods of relating to adults within the school. Chapter 12, the final chapter of both the section and the text as a whole, addresses classroom and school-based research for evidence-based decision-making.

Acknowledgements

The writers of this text have been working together in different capacities as course tutors, researchers, report writers and co-authors for a number of years. When we set out to write this text we determined to draw on a wide range of sources that included experience from our many collaborative ventures rather than merely offering a text that contained an overview of recent writing on the topic of middle leadership in primary schools. For this reason the text contains vignettes or case studies drawn from a number of sources, including research on Beacon schools, interviews with school leaders for a number of articles reconceptualizing school leadership and the reflections and experiences of long-standing friends and colleagues who hold relevant positions in primary schools in a number of locations in England. Many of these colleagues stated that they wished to remain anonymous or that, while they did not mind being named themselves, they did not wish to have their schools, colleagues and pupils identified. For this reason we wish to offer a general note of thanks to those who contributed to the writing of this text, either by consenting to be interviewed or by agreeing to submit their reflections on their experiences as middle managers in primary schools. Such contributors are all valued colleagues, some are long-standing friends.

While writing this text the authors were employed, respectively, at the University of Manchester Centre for Educational Leadership and De Montfort University School of Education. We would like to thank the staff and leaders of these departments and institutions for their support. It is one of the joys and responsibilities of academic life that we continue to write books and articles that both inform and support colleagues in schools and question, interrogate and elucidate educational policy-making. We hope that this text performs both these functions and we are, as writers and academics, both grateful that we have the time and space within busy work schedules to perform these tasks. To a large extent this sense of space to write is created by the diligence and hard work of other colleagues who administer, co-ordinate and facilitate the programmes on which we work and who take on many of the day-to-day duties involved in research, editorships and the other tasks that form the life of academics. For this reason we would like to thank Neesha Patel of the University of Manchester Centre for Educational Leadership.

Most of all we would like to thank our wives for their care and support, for their help in what can be the nightmarish world of lost reference finding, for their diligence in finding mislaid books and articles, and for their general tolerance and understanding.

Mark Brundrett and Neil Burton
2005

SECTION A

An Overview of the Components

1

Introduction: in search of subject leadership

LEARNING OUTCOMES OF THIS CHAPTER

By the end of this chapter you should be able to:

- understand the role of subject leadership in primary schools
- recognize the key attributes of the effective classroom practitioner
- articulate the overlapping roles of subject specialist, co-ordinator, consultant, manager and leader

The evolution of subject leadership in primary schools

For the best part of a century there has been an expectation that primary school headteachers will delegate responsibility for aspects of the management of the curriculum to teachers with particular areas of expertise or interest. Unlike secondary schools where, with a few notable exceptions, the whole organizational management has been based around subjects taught by well defined teams, which led naturally to the identification of promoted posts to assume responsibility for delegated duties, primary schools had, by and large, generalist teachers whose prime focus was defined by the age of the child. Subject leaders in secondary schools can normally rely upon having a well defined, often exclusive to the subject, group of teachers to work with. In primary schools, the key allegiance is to the year group or key stage, depending upon the size of the school.

The advent of the National Curriculum in 1989 (NCC, 1989) firmly organized the curriculum to be taught in primary schools along subject rather than age-focused lines, following the secondary rather than primary model of school organization. Much of the subsequent revisions and guidance offered by government-instituted bodies has reinforced this structural model. The notion of 'subject specialism' was further reinforced by the requirement, during the 1990s, that all new primary entrants to the teaching profession must qualify through receiving specialist knowledge in at least one of the National Curriculum subjects (DES, 1989) to an 'undergraduate' level. Qualification as a primary teacher via postgraduate qualified teacher status (QTS) routes was limited to those who could demonstrate that their degree was mostly or wholly within a subject taught within the primary school (DFE, 1993).

In this 'initiative rich' era, it became imperative, if primary schools were to comply with the newly established demands of the National Curriculum, that responsibility for initiating these changes needed to be devolved to individual members of the teaching staff, with the backing and support of the headteacher. This imperative continues only with the additional dimensions (or *complications?*) of issues and initiatives which require management and leadership but span across strict subject boundaries, such as literacy, gifted and talented children, and staff development. To be successful, the person responsible requires appropriate skills and knowledge in two distinct fields: generic leadership and management; and subject/responsibility specific. It is possible to map the development within these fields to understand better the nature of the role and progression towards proficiency and effectiveness in it. Figure 1.1 is a representation of the potential routes of development towards and beyond the role of 'subject leader'. Each of these steps will be examined and characterized in terms of the differential nature of the roles.

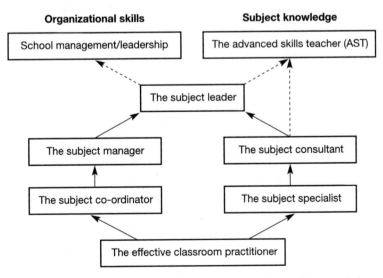

Figure 1.1 Potential routes of development towards and beyond the role of subject leader

The different approaches to the role were acknowledged, formally, by the TTA (1998) who defined the co-ordinator as a mainly reactive role and that of the subject leader as a proactive role. Bell and Ritchie (1999: 12) amplified this distinction further and clarified the work of past authors in the field by separating the *post* of the subject leader; the *responsibilities* that comprise the job description; and the *roles* that they perform in order to meet their responsibilities, which can be broken down into individual *tasks*. Essentially these distinctions suggest a different order of operation, the suggestion being that they reflect a difference in the internal structure of schools. An alternative perspective, the one taken here, is that these different roles represent developmental pathways and so represent indistinct points on a continuum between classroom teacher and subject leader. Indeed, the model above offers alternative routes dependent upon the relative strengths of the candidate. Prior to progressing towards leadership roles, we must establish and clarify the base reference point.

The effective classroom practitioner

Before progressing to having additional organizational roles within a school it is important to have the security of working from the basis of being a confident and effective classroom practitioner. Here the aim is to provide the best possible learning environment and opportunities for the children within the class, working within the constraints and towards the goals of the school.

To achieve effectiveness in the classroom a teacher will need to demonstrate significant understanding of, and the ability to apply, knowledge from five distinct areas:

1 *Subject knowledge*: demonstrating understanding of the nature and conceptual focus of the subjects to be taught.
2 *Curriculum knowledge*: a sound appreciation and confident application of the National Curriculum (DfES, 2004a), schemes of work (QCA, 2004) and their interconnectivity (DfES, 2003).
3 *Pedagogic knowledge*: the ability to apply the most appropriate teaching strategies to enhance learning.
4 *Pupil knowledge*: understanding of the strengths and needs of children in the classes being taught so as to be able to construct appropriate learning opportunities.
5 *Organization knowledge*: to be able to arrange and structure time and resources to be able to deliver appropriate learning opportunities.

By knowing and appreciating relative strengths in these areas, a teacher should be able to gain an indication of the most suitable direction he or she might progress in. If his or her strengths lie in the first three areas of knowledge, then it is likely that by maintaining a subject focus he or she could successfully enhance his or her career by progressing up the right-hand side of Figure 1.1. If strengths are apparent in the final three knowledge areas, then it is likely that the teacher has a more 'organizational' bias, and so would be more likely to progress along the route suggested by the left-hand side of Figure 1.1.

While curriculum knowledge is an integral element of all initial teacher education (ITE) courses, teachers will almost inevitably be more comfortable teaching in some areas rather than others. There will almost certainly be a direct link between these subjects, or combinations, and their own academic strengths – either through their first degree, followed by postgraduate teacher training, or the 'subject specialist' element of their undergraduate QTS course. However, a successful learner does not always equate to a successful teacher! A teacher who has overcome difficulties in learning a particular subject may find that he or she excels in teaching it, as he or she is more aware of the conceptual difficulties and misunderstandings that children may have than, say, a teacher who found the subject relatively easy to understand and has difficulty appreciating the problems that some children may be having. While at the beginning of a teaching career it will be the academic qualifications that will signal the subject specialism of the teacher, how this specialism impacts in the classroom will become the main determinant.

Pedagogy, the ability to select and employ appropriate teaching strategies to ensure that sustained and coherent learning takes place, must be the foundation of the profession. Whichever career path is chosen there needs to be this prerequisite to gain the trust and confidence of fellow teachers. Essentially the process of teaching is akin to the management of change – the assessment of the current situation, the identification and dissemination of targets, the selection of appropriate strategies, the monitoring and the evaluation are all crucial to the success of teaching and can all be translated into a management focus (see later chapters).

The deeper, empathic, abilities of some teachers that allow them to gain insight into the specific needs and (possibly untapped) strengths of individual children should be appreciated as a major asset. As with the pedagogic skills, it hints at the ability effectively to manage, lead and motivate adults as well as children – suggesting well placed, generic management skills are present, waiting to be developed in a wider range of contexts beyond the classroom.

Finally, those teachers who lead classrooms to be well organized, with clear systems and structures which all the children understand and can work to, are also demonstrating managerial skills that are highly desirable within the primary school. Clearly there are questions of ownership of the systems and structures that need to be asked to ensure that the characteristics are transferable, but the basic skills should be sound.

To an extent, these skills can be seen as being contextual. While a teacher may have the potential to achieve, he or she also needs to be given the opportunity – which may be, for example, a factor of management structure and culture, resources, school focus or pupil expectation. Teachers who have strengths in all these knowledge areas should have more options open to them in their choice of career development patterns. Indeed, to progress towards senior management within a primary school, it should be seen as essential that candidates have demonstrated strengths in all these areas!

ASK YOURSELF

- ◆ Where do I perceive my strengths to lie?
- ◆ What evidence can I offer in support of this perception?
- ◆ On which developmental route do I lie?

The subject specialist

As suggested above, in the early stages of career development, specialism may be indicated by academic qualifications, but for this to be sustained there needs to be reinforcement through classroom practice and pupil outcomes. To be considered a 'subject specialist' the teacher will need to demonstrate a 'flair' for the subject. This will manifest itself in one (or preferably more) of three ways:

1 *Observable classroom practice*: as part of the professional development and support practices within the school there should be a programme of classroom observation, in addition to more informal 'visits' from senior staff. Either formal criteria (Ofsted, 2004) or more informal perceptions of high-quality effective practice could be offered as evidence.

2 *Evidence of effective learning*: although various measures of educational value added may provide a reinforcement of the longer-term effectiveness of the teaching, more presentational formats may be more immediately informative (e.g. displays, assembly presentations, senior management review of pupils' books).

3 *Subject-specific support for colleagues*: either through specific shared planning or via *ad hoc* support for a less confidence colleague, a teacher may make a significant contribution to the quality of teaching beyond his or her own classroom.

There is an expectation that this point would be achieved within the first two to five years of teaching, depending upon the availability of opportunities. Many schools rely on appointing new entrants to the profession to act as 'agents of change' and to refresh the school through new approaches and attitudes to classroom practice. In the first couple of years of a primary teaching career, a teacher might be expected to 'shadow' a subject leader so that he or she can begin to appreciate the role in greater depth and perform some of the more 'administrative' duties attached to the post.

There is much to support the idea of leadership by example – it is the basic tool of behaviour management in almost every classroom in the land – but stepping up from the classroom to the school does require careful thought and engineering of opportunities. Mentoring during the NQT year should ensure that the classroom is visited frequently, providing ample opportunities for demonstration of teaching technique. In terms of the second point above, there needs to be thought as to how the quality of your teaching of your specialist area can be best presented to the school. Some of the more aesthetic subjects (music, art, dance, etc.) lend themselves to public displays, either static (classroom or entrance hall display) or dynamic (assembly presentation). Others may need to be presented in ways which rely more on display or drama skills than the subject of the specialism.

ASK YOURSELF

- ◆ What is my specialism, my area of excellence?
- ◆ What opportunities do I have to demonstrate my expertise?
- ◆ How can I make public the excellent work in my classroom?

The subject co-ordinator

This role has arisen out of the cult of the generalist primary teacher, so prevalent in the 1970s and early 1980s in England. Such a post was often held by a resource organizer responsible either for a particular subject area or for an important task within the school (such as 'display'). As such, these posts tended to be awarded on the basis of organizational skills rather than subject knowledge. Bell and Ritchie (1999: 12) list the 'underplay of expertise' as one of the core characteristics but this belies the reality of the appointment of posts of responsibility for subjects within primary schools. Primary schools tend to appoint most teaching staff on the basis of the quality of their teaching, with subject specialism being a further consideration. Given that the majority of English primary schools have five or fewer teachers, then appointing sufficiently multi-specialist teachers with exactly the right combination of subjects to match the ten subjects of the National Curriculum (DfES, 2003) (plus have specialisms in the appropriate age ranges within the school) would be little more than a minor miracle!

A subject co-ordinator, while having an enthusiasm for the subjects, is unlikely to have the in-depth background of the subject specialist. Effectively, a teacher will be asked to apply his or her classroom organizational skills to a whole-school role. The post-holder will be expected to perform many of the administrative tasks (such as ordering and organizing resources) of the subject leader but will be expected to call upon external support, in the form of subject specialist advisory teachers or private consultants, for advice and guidance on subject-specific matters.

Given this background, it is unlikely that such a post-holder will attempt to initiate any particularly dynamic changes from the current level and style of provision – he or she is much more likely to adopt a 'holding brief'. What the role-holder will bring to the position is the ability to organize and structure the provision for the subject within the school. Good classrooms run on an effective and efficient bureaucracy where all the members of the class understand and follow the systems and structures that have been put in place, knowing that they work and make the classroom a good and relatively stress free place to be. Teachers who develop and maintain such classrooms are ideal candidates to be installed as co-ordinators. Senior management can feel quite confident that, if they provide the new co-ordinator with the appropriate subject-specific documentation (suppliers, advisory staff, etc.) and appropriate support to initiate administrative changes where necessary, the subject will be in 'safe' hands.

A subject co-ordinator will fare best in a situation where the teaching staff are generally confident in their classroom practice and overall pupil outcomes are good, but just need to ensure that the resources and learning support materials are available.

ASK YOURSELF

- ◆ How well organized is my classroom?
- ◆ What systems and structures do I use in the class to make it run smoothly?
- ◆ How can I develop this approach for the benefit of the whole school?

The subject consultant

While the 'specialist' is in the early stages of proving his or her value to the school in terms of his or her expertise, the 'consultant' has progressed within the school to become the 'acknowledged resident expert'. In this role, he or she will be sought out and consulted on matters concerning his or her specialist subject by other members of the staff. Primarily consultants will be able to offer advice on the nature of the subject and its interconnectivity with the rest of the curriculum – both in terms of how it enhances and how other subjects enhance it – and support for planning, teaching and assessing/evaluating the subject. There is likely to be reactive and proactive elements within this approach. While there may be patches within the school where practice has significantly progressed due to the involvement and enthusiasm of the consultant, there may also be classrooms where practice has been relatively untouched – mainly dependent upon the initiative of those teachers to become involved. Essentially, what distinguishes the 'consultant' from the 'leader' is the ability to initiate and lead change systematically across the whole school.

Generally the consultant will work in the staffroom, providing support and advice on an *ad hoc* basis to those who ask which leads to improvements in learning and teaching for whole-class or group activities or identifying strategies for individual children with particular conceptual difficulties. Additionally the consultant may work beyond his or her own classroom on a class-swap basis to share expertise more widely throughout the school, or team teach so that both class and teacher gain the benefit of the expert teaching. There is also the option of bringing teachers into the consultant's classroom in order for them to observe best practice though model lessons.

Clearly the consultant is beginning to scale up the positive impact of his or her expertise within the school and, while he or she is likely to improve the quality of learning and teaching, it will be very much linked to his or her enthusiasm and passion for teaching the subject, rather than his or her organizational abilities. This strongly suggests the professional development that consultants need to participate in should be directed towards the development of management and leadership skills, such as school management programmes offered by various universities and 'Leading from the Middle' (NCSL, 2003).

An alternative line of development that a consultant may wish to consider is progression towards becoming an AST (advanced skills teacher) (DfES, 2004b) or moving into an advisory capacity within a local authority.

The subject manager

Where the difference between subject specialist and consultant was largely a matter of self-confidence in the content and teaching of the subject and the widening acceptance of expertise by the staff, so it is between co-ordinator and manager. A subject manager will have a more finely tuned set of management skills and strategies and will be able to apply them more appropriately and confidently within the school. There will be a greater level of trust exhibited by colleagues and an acknowledgement of his or her leadership potential.

It is worthy of note that *subject* manager may be a little misleading, as a person possessing and effectively deploying management level skills should be capable of managing many diverse, high-priority initiatives within the school, particularly those in which he or she has an interest. So important functions, as deemed by the school, such as assessment, recording and reporting or timetabling (in larger primary schools) may be devolved to a manager to organize and oversee.

A manager will have developed his or her organizational skills to a point where he or she is able to apply appropriate managerial strategies to address most problems. There will be a developing ability to assess the current situation and choose an appropriate strategy or structure to achieve the goals that have been set working within the limits of resources, time and personnel available. This ability to achieve desirable outcomes is more likely to be well established in situations where there is a fairly stable cultural environment – the manager will be more secure in the knowledge of which staff he or she is able to work with and which approaches/strategies are likely to be effective.

While the direction of development for consultants on the way to becoming subject leaders was clearly focused around management and leadership skills, it is not quite so straightforward for managers. They already possess many of the necessary organizational and managements skills, but they still need to develop their leadership potential. Anecdotally the difference between management and leadership can be expressed as:

- *management*: doing things right (a structures and systems focus); and
- *leadership*: doing the right things (a communications and vision focus).

Conceptually they are significantly different, and leadership is not a simple extension of a management function. Managers make things happen, but they need leaders to tell them what needs to happen; they need to work to a vision, a goal. Much of this 'knowing what needs to happen', the setting of the vision, is a result of applying specialist knowledge – and if we are considering leading a subject, then it is subject specialist knowledge that is required.

Developing a specialist knowledge, particularly in a subject of the National Curriculum, is a significant achievement, especially if it has not already been achieved by this point of a teaching career. There are two options that might be considered: either specializing in a cross-curricular issues (such as learning and teaching strategies or quality assurance issues) or making effective use of external consultants to help identify needs and set a vision for improvement.

ASK YOURSELF

- How do I organize people and resources to make things happen?
- What strategies do I employ to encourage individuals to adapt to new ways of working?
- Which aspects of school life am I most confident in managing?

The subject leader

In this role, the two strands of development presented in the model above (Figure 1.1) combine and significantly enhance each other. The development of leadership skills provides the subject specialist with the means of enacting and leading through change to improve the quality of learning and teaching throughout the school. Rather than leading by the example set in his or her own classroom and hoping for a ripple effect, the subject leader is able to rationalize the nature of his or her own effectiveness and present this as a model for the rest of the school to follow. The subject-specific knowledge provides the leader with the vision and direction to progress in.

The organizational traits in the professional make-up of subject leaders will allow them to take a more strategic view of developments and adopt a more innovative stance to achieve long-term gains based around the development of staff. It is important to note that the 'strategic view' taken above needs to balance various, often conflicting, perspectives and pressures. The aims and objectives of the school, according to the TTA (1998: 4), need to be met at the same time as those of the subject.

The subject leader must ensure that the direction the school is progressing in does not diverge from the national perspective offered by the subject – indeed, this being one subject among many that a school will need to accommodate within its vision. This balance between the internal and external expectations can be captured within the subject policy adopted by the school. The policy will need to reflect both the ethos and approach to learning and teaching within the school and the nature of the subject.

Judging the effectiveness of a subject leader presents some interesting issues as the many stakeholders in the school may hold different views on the matter and judge by different criteria. Ultimately it is the children who have the final say – the extent to which they enjoy, enthuse about and achieve in the subject. This will be used by others as their means of gauging success. The subject leader will have a significant influence over the nature and structure of the taught curriculum from the point of planning, resource and time allocation. The quality of the teaching will be strongly influenced by the skill with which teaching and classroom support staff are supported and trained. Means of monitoring and supporting the development of individual children will be developed and managed by the subject leader, as will the means by which learning targets for individuals and classes are set, monitored and valued.

External inspection will be of value to the academic progress of the children and the quality of the learning and teaching. Senior management (including governing bodies) will value the contribution that the subject makes to the life of the school and its overall priorities. Parents will value the enjoyment and interest that their children show in the subject and the success and personal development that they gain from it.

To progress beyond subject leadership the options are either to focus on the subject element, which leads into AST and subject advisory work, or the leadership skills, where the advancement can be into senior management within the primary school. Due to the nature of the National Curriculum, as it is currently constructed, it is inevitable that subject leaders in maths and English (numeracy and literacy!) will tend to have a more exalted position in the school hierarchy than other subject leaders. Given the emphasis placed on pupil proficiency and progress in these areas in the external inspection process and the annual round of target-setting, it is perhaps wholly understandable. However, in many cases it may be due to this additional responsibility that the most experienced leaders are placed in those positions.

While there are considerable external pressures to focus on the leadership of subjects as the basis of the management structure within the primary school, there is still the legacy of the 'child centred' approach to learning which persists from pre-National Curriculum days and is, in many ways, regaining favour through a renewed interest in learning technologies (accelerated learning, learning styles, etc.) and the influence of the 'primary strategy' (DfES, 2003). This had led schools to reconsider their leadership and management structures, offering leadership roles and responsibilities which focus primarily upon cross-curricular issues in order to emphasize the holistic educational development of individual children rather than their development within subject strands.

Summary

Although there are generic elements, the subject knowledge route to subject leadership will have many unique features dependent upon the subject. Many of the subject associations supporting the work of teachers in British primary schools have extremely useful resources to help individual teachers progress along those lines. The alternative route, to build upon good organizational systems and structures developed within the classroom and enhance them towards developing leadership qualities beyond the classroom, has the potential to offer more opportunities for advancement. Being less contextually focused, especially in terms of a subject focus, there tends to be fewer support mechanisms in place.

By mapping personal development to the stages outlined in Figure 1.1 it may be easier to identify where strengths and development opportunities lie. The remainder of Section A explores the potential to transfer classroom-based skills and strategies into the context of management and leadership opportunities within the primary school. Sections B–D then explain how those skills can be developed further to enable progression through to subject leader status.

References

Bell, D. and Ritchie, R. (1999) *Towards Effective Subject Leadership in the Primary School*. Buckingham: Open University Press.

DES (Department for Education and Science) (1989) *24/89 Initial Teacher Training: Approval of Courses*. London: HMSO.

DfE (Department for Education) (1993) *Circular 14/93: The Initial Training of Primary School Teachers*. London: HMSO.

DfES (Department for Education and Skills) (2003) *Excellence and Enjoyment – a Strategy for Primary Schools*. London: HMSO (online at http://www.dfes.gov.uk/primarydocument).

DfES (Department for Education and Skills) (2004a) *The National Curriculum for England*. London: HMSO (online at http://www.nc.uk.net/index.html).

DfES (Department for Education and Skills) (2004b) *Advanced Skills Teachers* (online at http://www.standards.dfes.gov.uk/ast/).

NCC (National Curriculum Council) (1989) *A Framework for the Primary Curriculum*. York: NCC.

NCSL (National College for School Leadership) (2003) *Leading from the Middle* (online at http://www.ncsl.org.uk/index.cfm?pageid=ldev-emer-gent-leading).

Ofsted (2004) *Inspecting your School*. London: HMSO (online at http://www.ofsted.gov.uk/publications/index.cfm?fuseaction=pubs.sum-mary&id=3662).

QCA (Qualification and Curriculum Authority) (2004) *Schemes of Work*. London: HMSO (online at http://www.standards.dfes.gov.uk/schemes3/).

TTA (Teacher Training Agency) (1998) *National Standards for Subject Leaders*. London: TTA (online at http://www.tta.gov.uk/php/read.php?sec-tionid=103&articleid=519).

Websites

National College for School Leadership, (2003) Leading from the Middle (http://www.ncsl.org.uk)

Teachernet (2005) Professional and Career Development (http://www.teachernet.gov.uk/development/)

2

The effective classroom practitioner

LEARNING OUTCOMES OF THIS CHAPTER

By the end of this chapter you should be able to:

- recognize the transferable skills that can be brought to the role of middle leader
- understand the importance of medium-term planning, lesson planning, implementation, and exposition of the curriculum
- describe and analyse the issues associated with behaviour management, evaluation, target-setting, planning for differentiation and diversity, and classroom resource management

Transferable skills

In the previous chapter the model of the effective classroom practitioner was outlined as the basis for development towards subject leadership. Many of the skills developed by teachers as a result of teaching classes of children can be transferred to school management and leadership contexts. This chapter explores the potential of some of these teacher-developed skills and looks forward to later chapters where they will be developed further.

ASK YOURSELF

- Which classroom-developed skills could be transferred to other contexts?
- What skills have I developed as a teacher?
- How might I make use of them in other contexts?

Professional development as a teacher relies heavily on the ability to transfer skills from one context to another – it is at the heart of reflective practice. Lessons that are learnt working with one group of children are reflected upon and applied to the next group. Where an approach to learning is found to be effective, it will be used again in another situation; where it isn't as effective as expected it will be amended or changed in a cycle of trial and success.

In schools (and colleges and universities for that matter) teachers have always been promoted as the managers and leaders of teachers and therefore the schools that they work for. In the commercial world there has always been the practice of employing managers and leaders who have previously found success in other business sectors. They are employed for their management and leadership qualities which are understood to be of greater value and importance than their understanding of the workings of the particular industry or company – that can be learnt through effective induction. Similarly, schools will appoint managers and leaders from other schools – they have an understanding of schooling, but will have a limited understanding of *this* particular school. In each case skills will need to be transferred from other contexts and applied to a new situation – with the jump being greater on some occasions than on others.

The transition to managing and leading in primary schools from managing and leading in a non-school context (i.e. moving to teaching as a second career) offers no direct transfer of skills and such transfer has always been seen as the exception. A scheme in Israel to fast track ex-military officers into principalship of secondary schools has proved to be a significant success. The organizational and leadership skills gained from their military experience are contextualized in the first year of transition, where the candidates train as teachers, and then in the second they are put into practice as they train and are mentored to headship. While they are required to lead their schools with a deputy who has responsibility for the curriculum, all other aspects of the leadership of the school, from resource management and public relations to vision-setting and motivating staff, are fully the concern of the principal. Indeed, studies (Schneider, 2002) have shown that the transition required is of the same scale as for a teacher progressing to headship. Whilst many would raise questions about the importation of 'military' values into schools such a scheme does suggest that a wealth of experience exists in the wider community that could be used in schools.

Teachers have to consider not only the skills that they have developed within the classroom that they might be able to apply to wider, whole-school situation, but also those appropriate skills that they have developed in other contexts. In particular it is important that those who have gained experience in a career prior to entering teaching fully appreciate the value of what they can bring to the school.

Learning lessons from the classroom

To be effective in the classroom teachers need to demonstrate a wide range of diverse skills and be able to deploy appropriate strategies to ensure a vibrant learning environment and enthusiastic, gainfully employed pupils. With experience these skills become embedded and are employed without conscious thought – this is a dangerous stage for a learner as comfort can suppress reflection and further development. In this section, the range of skills that a teacher routinely deploys in the classroom which can be further developed for a wider school use will be identified for further, more detailed examination below.

The primary purpose of teachers is to teach – and this is made possible by a number of inter-related activities:

- *Medium-term planning*: designing a developmental process taking pupils from their current state of learning to a higher, more desirable one.
- *Lesson planning and implementation*: presenting pupils with activities in which learning will take place, and linking this learning to previous experiences and what is to follow.
- *Exposition*: careful and considered explanation of tasks and expectations using language appropriate to the pupils.
- *Behaviour management*: encouraging behaviours in pupils that will make them more able to learn effectively and contribute positively to the learning of others.
- *Assessing learning and evaluating teaching*: monitoring progress towards planned outcomes to inform future action.
- *Target-setting*: identifying appropriate criteria by which to measure the success of learning.
- *Planning and teaching for differentiation and diversity*: acknowledging the different learning styles of pupils and adapting teaching appropriately.
- *Classroom resource management*: effective use of the learning environment and resources to enhance the potential for learning.

While there are many more key skills that could be identified, these have been chosen as they offer good access to the management and leadership skills that need to be developed as subject leaders within the primary school.

- ◆ Which of those areas do I excel in?
- ◆ How might I apply those skills to management situations outside the classroom?
- ◆ Which skills would I have chosen beyond the ones listed?

Medium-term planning

Essentially, medium-term planning consists of three elements. Knowing:

1 where you (the class of children) are;
2 where you want to get to (the aims/objectives); and
3 how to get there (the tasks that will provide the opportunities to learn).

Much of the medium-term planning that currently exists in English primary schools is derived from the QCA (2004) *Schemes of Work*, which provide a good model of practice as long as they are contextualized to the school and class in which they will be used. Being an effective practitioner means actually performing the planning rather than importing generic documentation from elsewhere. The process of planning for learning is conceptually very similar to planning for change (in an organizational and structural sense). Once the approach is mastered, it can be reapplied to other contexts.

The basic requirements of the process start with an accurate assessment of the current position – what the pupils already know and can do, in the case of planning for learning. This is then followed by a realistic prediction of what can be achieved (given the constraints of resources, ability, time, etc.) – the desired 'future position'.

Figure 2.1 provides a graphical representation of possible routes towards attaining the future position. There is normally more than one way of achieving the desired outcome (Figure 2.1 suggests three), and it is the task of the effective practitioner to choose the most appropriate one. The routes should be seen as indicators to track that appropriate progress is being achieved – objectives leading towards the overall aims. Alternatively, since the outcome is the same for all, it would be possible for different groups to achieve the same outcome by different means (each, possibly, addressing a different learning style).

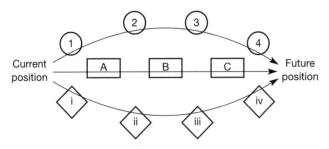

Figure 2.1 A graphical representation of possible routes towards attaining the future position

Clearly the model is flawed – seldom is the starting position the same for all, nor are they expected to achieve precisely the same outcome – but it does offer a useful simplification of the entire process. As with pupils beginning a new scheme of work, teachers embarking on a new initiative will find themselves in different states of preparedness and preparation and, almost inevitably, the teachers will emerge at the other end of the process with greater or lesser degrees of competence.

A revised model would start by acknowledging the lowest level of current competence and would identify the minimum acceptable future position. The more able or more initially advanced could then be collected along the way and be encouraged to exceed the minimum expectations. This differentiated approach can be seen in the model planning offered by the QCA (2004).

A further flaw in the model expressed in Figure 2.1 is the inference of sequential progression towards the aims. It is just as likely that there will be parallel activities/objectives that need to be achieved before further progression can be made but these can be approached in any order (see Figure 2.2). A further scenario might be that some will be able to progress sequentially but others, following the first activity/objective, require additional input to achieve the next stage. Or, finally, there may be alternative means of achieving the next step (denoted by '2a' and '2b').

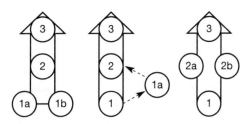

Figure 2.2 Parallel activities/objectives that need to be achieved before further progression can be made

- To what extent is my medium-term planning specific to my class?
- How deeply do I consider the purposes of my planning?
- Do I apply the planning processes, however informally, to other contexts?

Lesson planning and implementation

Whereas the section above was concerned with planning for change, this section is about leading through the implementation, stage by stage. Lesson planning and internal structure break down the planned-for development in the scheme into meaningful and manageable segments. Lessons are usually constructed in four sections:

1 *Location*: where the 'big picture' is examined and the lesson is placed in the context of what came before and what is to follow.
2 *Introduction*: the explanation of the content, focus and expectations for the session.
3 *Teaching focus*: class, group and individual activities designed to provide the pupils with opportunities to rehearse and demonstrate their learning.
4 *Plenary*: reinforce learning and recap on main teaching points and look ahead to future sessions.

Planning for and leading an individual staff training session as part of a larger, longer-term initiative will be very similar. Locating the training within the school development and improvement programme is essential in order to give the task gravity. It is important to avoid concentrating on 'information-giving' sessions – as with effective lessons, there needs to be some form of physical engagement with the task to allow participants to gain ownership. This does not mean that there has to be a 'doing' activity as part of the staff meeting (although much can be gained from this!) but there should be an element of 'go away, do (something) – preferably in groups or pairs – and bring back the results for the next session'. Joyce and Showers (1995) found that professional development through training activities was most likely to have the desired impact when it contained theory (why we are doing it), followed by demonstration (how we do it), followed by a period of practice (try it your self) and finally rounded off with feedback (let's evaluate how it went). So an input and focus session followed by a review and evaluation session would appear to be the ideal format for effective professional development using a 'staff meeting' approach.

Whatever the developmental focus (e.g. a revised reports format to clarify information given to parents and to simplify processes for staff), there needs to be clarity of 'why' followed by 'how', an opportunity to practice and the opportunity to review and be given constructive feedback. Without the review and feedback, Joyce and Showers (1995) found that the effectiveness of any training was greatly diminished.

ASK YOURSELF

- What are the characteristics of my best lessons?
- How might I contextualize the learning more effectively?
- How much do I change my approach to teaching when I work with adults?

Exposition

The clarity of the explanation of the task, the purpose of the learning, how it relates to other learning and the expectations can transform a well planned lesson in to an excellent learning experience. Effective, clear communication can significantly improve the success of an initiative and the chances of all staff acting in unison. One of the biggest causes of stress in primary schools (and education generally) is ambiguity – usually not knowing precisely what the focus and priorities of the school are, or having rapidly changed. In the way that pupils in the classroom can generally achieve if the expectations are appropriately clarified and reinforced, exactly the same it true of the staffroom.

It is true for both the classroom and the staffroom that there needs to be a shared understanding of the terminology to ensure that tasks can be effectively engaged in (stress free!). However, while strategies aimed at reinforcing and confirming shared understanding in the classroom are essential and appropriate, they need to be applied with great diplomacy and tact in the staffroom!

Essentially the language used in such situations needs to be constructive, positively framed and delivered with the expectation of compliance and co-operation. As a brief example, a request would not be accompanied with a 'please' (which assumes a 'pleading' position), but with a 'thank you' in anticipation of it being done. An effective exposition will clearly explain why where we want to be (the goal of the initiative or training) is so much better than where we currently are. It will connect with all the participants in a way that it gives the purpose meaning for them and encourages their support and engagement – it gives them ownership of both the problem (the current position) and the solution (the means of change) so that they can share the success of the outcome (the position that we want to be in).

A final important ingredient is the impact of non-verbal communication – what is the body or the face saying? Is it contradicting the words that are being spoken? Positive words will have limited success unless they are delivered in a confident tone with confident expressions. It is just as important to *look* as though you know what you are talking about as to sound as though you do!

ASK YOURSELF

- ◆ What language do I use?
- ◆ How important is my confidence in the subject?
- ◆ How clear am I about the message I am trying to convey in my explanations?

Behaviour management

One of the prime constituents of an effective classroom is the maintenance of behaviours appropriate to a learning environment. Clearly there is a diversity of behaviours which are effective for learning; different learners have differing styles of learning and different perspectives on what they regard as an environment conducive to learning. Effective teachers are able to manage these differences within the classroom to avoid, for the most part, behaviour becoming an issue. An ideal situation is where the teacher is not having to 'force' children to do something that they would rather not, but is able to engineer an environment where the children want to do the activity or task. To a large extent behavioural issues can be circumvented by ensuring that the lessons are well planned, engaging and appropriately challenging and by the teacher applying motivational techniques to encourage an enthusiastic response from the pupils.

Unfortunately it is not always possible to engage all the pupils all the time and additional strategies are required. Some can be applied to the whole class, such as the following:

- *Appropriate background music*: to encourage concentration and improve attention spans (Smith and Call, 1999).
- *Brain Gym*: using specially designed physical activities within the lessons to stimulate the ability to learn (Dennison and Dennison, 1998).

Other strategies may be required to target individuals who have developed non-standard responses to stimuli and encouragement. With these individuals it is often necessary to delve deeper into their psyche to understand their response mechanisms and develop appropriate strategies (see, for example, Hughes, 2004).

The ultimate goal of behaviour management strategies is to get classes and pupils to *want* to do what you want them to do. There is frequently a great deal of complex psychological interplay built around the positive effects of rewards and encouragement in order to achieve the desired outcomes and to construct a set of more desirable responses to situations through the examination of the consequences of potential alternative responses.

The ability to 'read' other individuals in order to choose the most appropriate strategies to encourage them to follow a 'preferred' path of action is an important skill to develop. It requires careful observation of body language and facial expression and careful listening not only to the words spoken but also to how they are delivered. With practice, the primary school teacher can become adept at reading the responses of the children in his or her class and so can make early interventions to avoid problems arising through behavioural mismanagement.

These behaviour management skills can be used, in modified forms, with adults to encourage and motivate them to engage in activities and complete tasks. Different colleagues within the school will be motivated by different strategies – while some thrive on praise, others will be inspired by challenge. The effective teacher will avoid the potential of behavioural problems by ensuring that the preparation for the session is secure. This is major lesson from the classroom that education managers need to apply – starting from a position of strength and confidence and maintaining consistency.

Where 'improper' or inappropriate behaviour needs to be managed, again the successful strategies developed in the classroom need to be applied – particularly the focus on the unwanted behaviour rather than the individual. Indeed, research by MacBeath (1998) suggested that, while managers in school would tend to let inappropriate behaviour or performance go, they themselves would want to know when they were doing something wrong so that they could rectify the situation.

Clearly there is a difference in position from being the classroom teacher and being a member of the teaching team. By being the teacher (and the adult!) there is an inbuilt assumption of authority within the classroom. Direct requests for action can be made more confidently from a position of authority, but it is also this confidence, not arrogance, that will encourage colleagues to be more compliant and responsive to requests from subject leaders. Section D of this book will explore the issues surrounding the motivation and leadership of staff in detail.

- ◆ Am I proactive or reactive to managing behaviour?
- ◆ What classroom strategies and systems do I operate to avoid behaviour becoming an issue?
- ◆ How do I positively and constructively respond to inappropriate behaviours?

Assessing learning and evaluating teaching

The effective practitioner should be locked into a reflective cycle of 'continuous improvement' (West-Burnham, 1992: 37) for personal and professional development. Experience should make it instinctive to a point of being an embedded process. Formal lesson evaluations help to focus the process and external stimuli can be used to offer a wider perspective and encourage a more radical approach to improvement. The assessment of learning is essential on two levels: first, to inform future planning for learning, for both individuals and whole classes; and, secondly, to judge the success of the teaching. So evaluation focuses on the process of teaching and assessment on the outcomes. Both these processes are integral to the effective management of change and improvement within the school.

While the setting of criteria to assess pupil outcomes by is now an integral part of lesson planning for all teachers, the means by which pupils will be able to demonstrate that they have met the learning objectives for the session, the evaluation criteria, can still be rather generic in nature. Due to this it might appear that assessment techniques are generally much more advanced than those focusing on self-evaluation.

Hardie (2001: 71), adapting the work of Stake (1976), suggests a bi-dimensional perspective of the assessment of learning for those leading the curriculum: a formative dimension that is developmental and diagnostic to inform ongoing professional development; and a summative dimension that stresses the end-product and is used more for evaluative purposes and to hold teachers and the school accountable. In the classroom, a teacher will have a wide range of assessment tools available, both formal and informal, designed to focus narrowly on pupil achievement in specific elements of subjects – with a particular emphasis on numeracy and literacy.

The criteria employed by Ofsted (2003) provide a clear focus for the inspection of the quality of learning and teaching but can only be applied through a judgemental process based upon experience and professional moderation. Ideally, self-evaluation of classroom performance and, to a certain extent, peer observation and review, should be guided by school policy and vision statements, given greater focus through school improvement targets.

Applying the skills and strategies employed in assessing pupils and self-evaluating teaching performance has already been alluded to above. Both skills are vital to the development of a subject across a school – they allow the subject leader to monitor progress and identify professional development needs. But in assessing samples of work produced by children in each of the classes, the subject leader can develop an appreciation of the level that the pupils are operating at. When this is compared with expectations for each age group, the subject leader will gain an indication of which classes are in particular need of support or teachers requiring professional development. A cycle of monitoring of planning and samples of pupils' work will provide an outline of the developmental work that needs to be done, but classroom observation, allowing for joint evaluation of teaching performance, will allow for the development of individualized training plans. In the same way that a teacher should be able to state a personal focus for a lesson alongside the objectives for the pupils, there should be a jointly agreed focus for any peer observation. General observations are fine as an orientation process, but there needs to be a clear focus if the observation is to be used as the basis of professional development, particularly if it is part of a coaching programme.

ASK YOURSELF

- ◆ Do I have a clear professional objective for each lesson that I use as the basis of my self-evaluation?
- ◆ Do I have a long-term view of self-evaluation for my own professional development?
- ◆ How do I know what to focus on when observing others?
- ◆ How do I share the outcomes of my lessons with other teachers?

Target-setting

Lately the whole of the public sector has been subjected to an almost obsessive emphasis on the use of target-setting as a means of predicting and improving performance. Teachers and schools are expected to use aggregated data to predict the performance of their pupils on the basis of their past achievements. There is still considerable debate about how the performance targets for pupils can be utilized most effectively to benefit the children and their long-term development.

Guidance from Teachernet (2003) focuses on the use of targets to inform stakeholders (parents, local community, etc.) on the overall performance of a school rather than inform on individual progression. However, Pupil Achievement Tracking (PAT) (DfES, 2004) allows the future performance of individual pupils to be predicted using aggregated data based upon the outcomes of standardized tests which can be administered by the school. In the case of primary schools this only accounts for target-setting in the areas of English and mathematics from the age of 7. If the performance of individuals is to be judged solely on the basis of such narrowly defined indicators, then there is the potential that talents in other fields will be undervalued, if not ignored.

In the classroom, effective teachers are continually setting performance targets, both short and long term. Lesson objectives are usually offered on at least three levels to provide appropriately challenging targets for children with different abilities. Targets are also frequently set on a weekly or half-termly basis focusing on the development of more general academic or social skills (such as sentence structure in written work or complying with requests first time).

It is important that these targets are used wisely – they need to be taken as indicators of performance rather than be taken as final outcomes alone. Just concentrating teaching effort on achieving the outcomes defined in the target will seriously impair the quality of the overall curriculum being offered to the pupils. Targets need to be adopted as indicators of underlying good practice – to all well set targets there is a qualitative as well as the quantitative element.

As a process it has many uses within educational management, not least in the management of teacher performance. To enact a good school improvement plan (SIP), the main thrust of development needs to be converted into meaningful targets for each member of staff. Subject leaders will play a key role in the development of the SIP.

The setting of individual targets can therefore be linked back to the previous section on evaluation of classroom performance – where they would offer direction and scope to the coaching or other forms of professional development offered. Further discussion of the use of target-setting as a means of managing subject and school improvement will be addressed in Chapters 4 and 11.

Planning and teaching for differentiation and diversity

While there is an abundance of evidence provided by the government (Ofsted, 2004; Teachernet, 2004) and various other sources, such as subject associations, focusing on approaches to learning and teaching that can lead to improved practice, teachers still need to contextualize the ideas to meet the specific needs of individuals within their classes. With the increasing emphasis on the need for teachers to understand the nature of learning, as the basis for developing an effective pedagogy, the focus on learning styles (Riding and Rayner, 1998), accelerated learning (Smith and Call, 1999) and multiple intelligences (Gardner, 1983; Goleman, 1996) has become increasingly intense. All approaches to the issue acknowledge the importance of valuing the diversity within the classroom and adapting teaching to encompass all styles to allow all pupils access to the substance of the lesson.

From the management or leadership perspective the lesson to be learnt here is that teachers and other staff, like children, have different learning strengths and weaknesses. The section above, 'Lesson planning and implementation', provides a basis for development, but in setting tasks and leading staff development there should be overviews/explanations in different formats – visual (e.g. flow charts or mindmaps), audio (e.g. verbal delivery) and kinaesthetic (e.g. physical resources). This should allow all staff access to the initial information. If there are tasks to perform, different groups could be encouraged to 'report back' using different presentation formats – diagrammatic, written lists, etc.

Where possible the subject leader, when apportioning tasks, should consider these differences and help by allowing individuals to work to their strengths within a team – where possible teams should be constructed to contain a balance of styles so that strengths and perspectives can be shared.

Differentiation is not just a matter of learning strengths but of experiences and expertise – as suggested in 'Medium-term planning' (above), there is a need to acknowledge that everybody is likely to be starting from a different place. From an effectiveness perspective it should be recognized that the ones who start from the lowest level of understanding or confidence are the ones that the school can least afford to leave behind.

Classroom resource management

Although the efficient management of resources within the classroom can be perceived as a rather low-level skill, in a situation where resources are in scarce supply savings in one area can be vired to provide extra resources elsewhere. Classrooms where pupils are encouraged to value their resources and equipment and use and store them carefully will tend to appear better resourced than classrooms where they are not – especially towards the end of the year. Apart from the social aspects of encouraging the pupils to take greater pride in their surroundings and their equipment, there is also the organizational bonus that the availability of resources improves the flow and success of lessons.

A well organized classroom teacher should be capable of making the step to co-ordinate a subject. By applying the approach to organizing and maintaining resources in the classroom to the resources for the subject in the school the teacher should be able to provide the means for teachers throughout the school to make effective use of what is available. Experience suggests that a teacher who has a classroom with a well used and vibrant library would be ideally placed to co-ordinate the school library. It is likely that the children in that class have been effectively inducted into good procedures and practices and could be given responsibility for organizing other classrooms.

Summary

In many cases teachers develop the necessary management and leadership skills as part of their classroom practice. Effective teachers are adept at multi-tasking – delegating, leading, motivating, monitoring, resource management, etc. – taking direct responsibility for the education of a group of children. Given this experience no teacher should fail or succumb to stress when accepting additional responsibilities for a subject across the school – but they do. Too frequently the skills that make them excellent classroom practitioners become too embedded within the particular context of the classroom and prevent them from effectively applying them to the wider school context. By being more aware of the skills that have been developed and how they have parallels in school management, the transition to a post of responsibility within the school can be made more confidently and successfully.

ASK YOURSELF

- ◆ Do I value the skills that I do have?
- ◆ Am I aware how experienced subject leaders apply their skills to their post?
- ◆ How do I begin to take a whole-school perspective for a subject?

References

Dennison, P. and Dennison, G. (1998) *Brain Gym: Simple Activities for Whole Brain Learning*, London: Body Balance Books.

DfES (Department for Education and Skills) (2004) *Pupil Achievement Tracker* (online at http://www.standards.dfee.gov.uk/performance/).

Gardner, H. (1983) *Frames of Mind*. London: Fontana.

Goleman, M. (1996) *Emotional Intelligence*. London: Bloomsbury.

Hardie, B. (2001) 'Managing monitoring of the curriculum', in D. Middlewood and N. Burton (eds) *Managing the Curriculum*. London: Paul Chapman Publishing.

Hughes, D. (2004) *Building Bonds of Attachment*. London: Rowman & Littlefield.

Joyce, B. and Showers, B. (1995) *Student Achievement through Staff Development: Fundamentals of School Renewal*. New York, NY: Longman.

MacBeath J. (ed.) (1998) *Effective School Leadership: Responding to Change*. London: Paul Chapman Publishing.

Ofsted (2003) *Inspecting Schools: Framework for Inspecting Schools*. London: HMSO (online at http://www.ofsted.gov.uk/publications/docs/hb2003/frame03/hmi1525-06.html#teaching).

Ofsted (2004) *Best Practice Cameos* (online at http://www.ofsted.gov.uk/schools/).

QCA (Qualification and Curriculum Authority) (2004) *Schemes of Work*. London: HMSO (online at http://www.standards.dfes.gov.uk/schemes3/).

Riding, R. and Rayner, S. (1998) *Cognitive Styles and Learning Strategies*. London: David Fulton.

Schneider, A. (2002) 'Understanding transition to principalship'. Unpublished research for PhD thesis, University of Leicester.

Smith, A. and Call, N. (1999) *The ALPS Approach: Accelerated Learning in the Primary School*. Stafford: Network Educational Press.

Stake, R. (1976) *Evaluating Educational Programmes*. Paris: OEDC.

Teachernet (2003) *Target Setting* (online at http://www.teachernet.gov.uk/management/atoz/t/targetsetting/).

Teachernet (2004) *Teaching and Learning: Case Studies* (online at http://www.teachernet.gov.uk/teachingandlearning/casestudies/).

West-Burnham, J. (1992) *Managing Quality in Schools*. Harlow: Longman.

Recommended reading

Middlewood, D. and Burton, N. (2001) *Managing the Curriculum*, London: Paul Chapman Publishing.

Websites

Hay McBer (2000) The Hay McBer model of teaching effectiveness (http://www.haygroup.co.uk)

3

From subject to curriculum

LEARNING OUTCOMES OF THIS CHAPTER

By the end of this chapter you should be able to:

- describe and analyse the relationship between subject and curriculum and articulate the key concepts contained within the idea of a curriculum
- articulate the factors that influence the development of the curriculum
- recognize the stakeholders in the curriculum and articulate the components that make up the curriculum

Subject and curriculum

While a subject may have a structure and internal coherence in its own right, it needs to be distilled into the form of a curriculum in order for it to be effectively taught in any systematic way. The concept of 'curriculum' has been the focus of much debate over many years and provides a literature which cannot be fully reviewed here. However, the distinction is important as the term preferred by the DFES is 'subject' rather than 'curriculum' leader (TTA, 1998). 'Curriculum' can be properly conceived as a subset of 'subject' in that it will offer only a partial coverage of the full range of knowledge and skills encompassed by the subject and it will offer a particular interpretation of the nature of the subject. It could be conceived that the role of the subject leader is to go beyond the confines of the defined curriculum, usually taken as being the 'National' Curriculum (NC) (DfES, 2004a), to ensure that the delivery maintains a wider perspective and an acknowledgement that the subject, and its applications, expands beyond the confines of the constructed curriculum.

It is important that the subject leader does not restrict his or her perspective of the subject he or she is leading to the boundaries of the NC. However, when developing a curriculum for a subject, the NC does offer an excellent starting place, having been constructed on the basis of evidence from many sources including those within the teaching profession, especially representatives from the relevant subject associations. Given that the original formulation of the NC in 1989 was based strictly around subjects, in order to emphasize the lines of conceptual and skill development, to be compatible with the prevailing approach to teaching in the secondary sector, there were some incompatibility issues in primary schools where a child-centred approach dominated. More recently the value of a holistic curriculum, or at least one that acknowledges the links and the need for consistency between subjects, has been promoted through a coherent 'primary strategy' (DfES, 2003).

This chapter therefore focuses on the need to contextualize the elements of the subject to be contained within the curriculum to make it relevant to the needs of the pupils and consistent with the approach to learning and teaching adopted by the school. It is the factors that influence this construction, both internal and external to the school, that are examined here.

The conceptual basis of the curriculum

In constructing a curriculum it would be all too easy to begin with the subject matter rather than framing the process within a coherent educational philosophy. By starting with the content of the curriculum it is likely that an underlying philosophy will become apparent as the construction process continues, reflecting the views of the authors. This approach is likely to lead to an overt (the planned or intended curriculum) and a covert (or 'hidden', in the words of Pollard and Tann, 1987) curriculum. While it would appear that two decades ago a covert curriculum, containing key skills and attitudes that were passed on to pupils as part of the culture of the school, could exist in an unacknowledged, hidden state, this practice should no longer be considered acceptable. If these values and attitudes are sufficiently important to be contained within the construction of the curriculum, they need to be overtly acknowledged and valued within the school. Indeed, it is these hidden, cultural elements that define the school and its philosophy for the education of children, and therefore need consistently to underpin *all* subjects taught in the school.

By raising the 'hidden curriculum' to the centre of the curriculum development process it can then be matched for consistency against the school's mission statement to focus the whole construction process rather than emerging from it. In this respect it is unfortunate that when the original versions of NC documentation for each subject were published, the emphasis was strongly focused on the need for teachers to develop the necessary subject knowledge to present to the pupils rather than develop an appreciation of the underlying philosophy on which the curricula were based. This problem was exacerbated by the need for primary teachers to come to terms with the demands of ten separate subject documents with little initial support from the DfES to map the consistencies and connectivity between them. It is only really since the turn of the century that sufficient confidence has returned, along with curriculum stability, to allow primary schools to move to a higher plain and concentrate on the philosophical overview rather than the technical compliance with the curriculum.

The work of Silcock and Brundrett will be examined in much greater detail in Chapter 11, but it is useful in the context of this initial discussion to note that they offer three models which exemplify the different stances taken by curriculum designers, including the following;

- A teacher or subject-centred ('top-down') approach, where a predetermined curriculum is delivered.
- A learner-centred ('bottom-up' approach), where the curriculum manager determines or designs the curriculum on the basis of student needs.
- A 'partnership' approach which seeks to bind teacher and learners to a common enterprise combining external expectations and individual needs (Silcock and Brundrett, 2001: 35).

All three models are points on a continuum from a child-centred to a centrally determined curriculum. In fact, it could be argued that Silcock and Brundrett do not go far enough, as the 'top-down' model still suggests ownership on the part of the teacher. But given that a centrally determined curriculum, such as early incarnations of the NC, is subject to interpretation through the process of teaching, it can be accepted as a reasonable interpretation of reality. In the mid-1980s the bottom-up model would have been very recognizable, but since then the influence of the NC has been so intense it would be hard to imagine the development of a curriculum without some form of external pressure.

If we assume that the reality is somewhere near the mid-point of this continuum, determined to a large extent by the self-confidence of the school, then we can begin to explore the conceptual structure of a curriculum in finer detail. Wragg conceptualizes a 'cubic curriculum', in which each dimension of the cube presents a discrete aspect of the curriculum:

1 The subject being taught (i.e. *what* is being learnt and taught).

2 Cross-curricular themes (i.e. *what* makes separate components into a whole).

3 The forms of teaching and learning employed (i.e. *how* everything is communicated) (1997: 3).

In many respects this model offered an excellent prediction of the current reality. The subject basis of the NC has now been effectively combined in the most developmentally advanced schools with the cross-curricular themes, underpinned by a secure understanding and implementation of revised approaches to learning and teaching, such as accelerated learning (Preedy, 2000). It is descriptive in nature, offering a means of perceiving the organization and emphasis in the developmental process.

Adopting a 'curriculum management' stance, Burton and Middlewood (2001: 19) also offer a model with three dimensions. The proposed dimensions are hierarchical in nature, from the philosophical to the practical:

1 visionary
2 strategic
3 structural.

At the 'vision' level the school offers educational leadership through a statement of what they want the pupils to learn – the skills, knowledge and attitudes that will define the cultural basis of the school. At the 'strategic' level the vision is translated into an operational taught curriculum, defined by the subjects' organization and the pedagogy through which they will be taught. At the structural level resources are identified and deployed (staff, teaching materials, etc.) to 'enable the taught curriculum to be delivered' (Burton and Middlewood, 2001: 19).

The Wragg model can be seen as being the strategic component of the Burton/Middlewood model. What the latter model calls for is a clear statement of purpose to express the direction and focus for the curriculum and then to underpin its delivery by confirming the appropriate deployment of resources.

The reality that we face is the gap between the planned curriculum and the received curriculum (see Figure 3.1). There has to be an acknowledgement that the individuality of every pupil will mean that they each learn something different, regardless of the uniformity of the taught curriculum. Each child will only assimilate a fraction of what was intended – success will be determined by how large that fraction is.

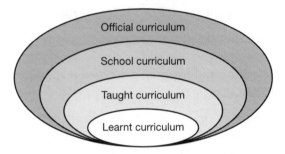

Figure 3.1 The gap between the planned and received curriculum

Each curriculum level might be regarded as a subset of the previous level – not all that is taught will be learnt; not all that the school plans for will be taught and so on. A best case scenario would be that the match is almost complete and curricula will not be perfect subsets – e.g. there will be elements taught that are not part of the school's planned curriculum for the subject.

It is important for the subject leader to understand not only what is taught but also why. Stepping back to take a wider view of the curriculum does not mean just to locate it within the nature of the subject, but also to locate it within the nature of the school. For that reason it is important to appreciate the influences on the nature of the school and schooling.

ASK YOURSELF

- ◆ At what level do I interact with the curriculum that I teach?
- ◆ What is the level of connectivity between my own personal philosophy for education, the school's policies and the values and aims of the National Curriculum (DFES, 2004b)?
- ◆ To what extent do I build upon the foundation of the National Curriculum in my planning?

Influencing the development of the curriculum

Wragg (1997) lists seven factors which influence the nature of the curriculum:

1 economic
2 technological
3 social
4 political

5 cultural
6 ideological
7 educational theory.

Each has national and local perspectives which may have either cumulative or counter-influences.

Economic factors

The government holds very clear views on the value of education within the economic development of the country: that 'our children are our future as a civilised and prosperous nation' (DfEE, 1997: 2), which it also expresses in the name the 'Department for Education and Skills'. Education is seen as investment in the human capital of the country, with an economy based upon high technology and communication – which is directed and focused through the demands of the National Curriculum. However this has led the primary sector to become very focused on targets based on measurable learning targets in 'basic' subjects rather than on instilling life-long learning skills needed for multi-career working lives.

Changing economic conditions also have significant impact on the supply of teachers, with graduate entry to the profession improving when graduate careers in other sectors of the economy become more difficult to sustain. There is also an increasing tendency for teaching to become a short-term rather than life-long career option.

For individual schools the realities of the local economic conditions can become very stark. Over the past 25 years, primary schools have come to rely on parental and community contributions as an additional source of income. School staff can be drawn into fundraising activities in order to provide resources for the curriculum that they want to deliver. Inevitably, schools in poorer areas tend to do less well at raising additional funds than those in more affluent communities. A 'sponsored' event in one school may realize sufficient funds to equip a computer suite, whereas the same event in a similar-sized school elsewhere may not even fund the purchase of a PC.

Expectations of what educational resources children have at home to support their school work will also vary tremendously – simply having books in the home may be more than can be hoped for. The level of home support for the educational development of children is significantly affected by economic factors such as the quality of housing, the stimulation provided by the local environment and the economic expectations of the home.

Technological factors

Information and communication technology (ICT) is at the heart of a learning revolution within British schools. Since the introduction of educational radio programmes in the 1920s, schools have embraced new media for communicating ideas and experiences. Ten years ago the National Curriculum for England prescribed that children aged 5–7 'should be taught to use IT equipment and software confidently and purposefully to communicate and handle information, and to support their problem solving, recording and expressive work' and that older pupils aged 7–11 'should be taught to extend the range of IT tools they use for communication, investigation and control; become discerning in their use of IT; select information, sources and media for their suitability for purpose; and assess the value of IT in their working practices' (DfE, 1995). But it is the confidence and competence of teachers in the use of this technology to enhance learning that need to be the focus for development if the potential is to be realized.

The sharing of expertise and resources between teachers and schools has been made possible through electronic communications; it makes it possible that pupils 'anywhere will be able to take the best courses taught by great teachers' (Gates, cited in Dryden and Vos, 2001: 458). The most effective, stimulating learning materials, produced almost anywhere in the world, can be used in your classroom to support your teaching – as subject leader, you need to find them and disseminate them within your school.

But using ICT in learning and teaching does not automatically lead to an improvement in educational quality and outcomes. Technology should not be used because it is there, but because it improves – and if it does not improve, it should not be used. For technology to enhance learning it requires several condition. To be:

- *available*: the hardware and software need to be accessible at the point of use;
- *stable*: the teacher needs to be confident that it will consistently perform as expected;
- *appropriate*: it needs to be contextually well matched to the needs of the learner; and
- *known about*: users need to be aware of what is available and what it can achieve.

Social factors

The value placed upon education is strongly influenced by the social background of teachers, pupils, parents and the local community. Those who
perceive themselves to have succeeded in their life aspirations as a result of
education are more likely to value education than those who have not. Not
only does the school need to provide a curriculum than convinces the pupils
of the values of learning and succeeding in education but it also needs to
convince the parents so that encouragement and support also come from
the home.

To be effective the curriculum will need to draw on the values held by the
learner, developing, enhancing and shaping them along the way. The school
will need to balance the sensitivities towards these values while encouraging
higher aspirations. There can be a wide difference in perceptions of 'normal-
ity' between teachers and pupils which needs to be addressed. Home support
for learning needs to take into account changes to the structure of the family
unit – with potentially less long-term security, lone-parent families, etc., the
use of education as a means of social engineering is addressed below.

Political factors

Vlaeminke (1998) points to the vital role of education, through the curriculum, in transmitting a cohesive national culture and in promoting national
identity either through what is directly taught or through the culture of the
school. Now that central government has strictly limited the level of influence that local politics can bring to bear on schools it is the national
perspective that impacts on the nature of the curriculum through the development of 'citizenship' (DfES, 2004a).

At the school level, the mission statement offers a means by which the
governing body and staff of the school can place in public record their perception of the value and focus that they intend to provide within the school.
By its very nature this will be a political statement: either by reinforcing the

views of the government by restating official policy, or by offering a local perspective by establishing a position based on the perceived educational needs of the local community.

Cultural factors

Schooling will inevitably involve the transmission of cultural values, particularly those of the staff employed by the school. If the cultural values of the staff come from a significantly different section of society than those of the pupils, their families and the local community, then there is the potential for misunderstanding, conflict and alienation. Not only is culture expressed through the content of the curriculum – the use of language, history, scientific viewpoints and so on – but also in the nature of learning and teaching. Children born into cultures with a strong oral tradition based upon allegorical stories may have difficulty accessing a curriculum based upon instruction and practical representation of learning. Due to the social location of women in some cultures, some pupils (and their families) might find it challenging when confronted with the predominantly female workforce in primary schools.

For the subject leader the challenge may be to find a means of valuing the perspective and input of pupils from a range of diverse cultures in a curriculum which is constructed around a national focus which attempts to value and celebrate the national heritage. Pupils may enter the school with value systems or worldviews which the intended curriculum does not take into account, making it difficult for the pupils to make connections between their learning in school and their wider knowledge and understanding base.

Different cultural groupings place significantly different values on education. Some cultures emanating from the Asian Pacific rim place a very high value on learning and education (Reynolds and Farrell, 1996), giving teachers a high social status and resulting in children from this cultural background performing better than national averages. Other cultural groups fare less well even where the curriculum takes their background more into account.

Ideological factors

What society perceives the purpose of schooling to be is complex and often confused by political rhetoric. Society offers clusters of beliefs, values and understandings which are combined to construct an ideology that defines what it is 'right' and 'natural' for pupils to do in primary schools. These ideologies vary from group to group, from individual to individual, but may be represented by one of the seven constructs shown in Table 3.1.

Table 3.1 Seven constructs of ideology

Ideology	Central values in respect of curriculum
Elementary	Curriculum is to meet society's economic and labour needs, and to preserve the existing social order. Education as a preparation for working life
Progressive	Curriculum is to enable the child to realize his or her full potential as an autonomous individual. Childhood a unique phase of development, not just a preparation for adulthood. Curriculum open and negotiable
Developmental	Curriculum is to be structured and sequenced in accordance with the child's psychological and physiological development and learning processes
Behavioural/ mechanistic	Curriculum is defined and structured in terms of hierarchies of observable and testable learning outcomes
Classical humanist	Curriculum is about initiating the child into the 'best' of the cultural heritage, defined chiefly in terms of disciplines or forms of understanding: the arts, sciences and humanities
Utilitarianism	Curriculum is to meet society's economic, technological and labour needs, to enable the child to adapt to changes in these, and to preserve the existing social order
Egalitarian	Curriculum to enable the child both to fulfil individual potential and to contribute to societal progress. The latter defined in terms of plurality, democracy and social justice, as well as the economy

Source: Alexander (1988).

ASK YOURSELF

- ◆ How do my values and perceptions influence my teaching?
- ◆ Are my values in line with those expressed by my school, or my pupils?
- ◆ What are the major influences on my educational values?

Influential stakeholders

There are a range of discrete groups or individuals who each have a greater or lesser impact on the nature of the curriculum being delivered in a school. While some, such as pupils and teachers, have an immediate and dynamic impact on the curriculum through the interaction in the classroom, others, for example the state and business and commerce, take a much longer-term, strategic view. This continuum is represented in Figure 3.2. Almost all teachers are products of the educational system they now work in, and their values and aspirations have been shaped by the classes they now teach in. Teachers need to avoid reproducing the education that they received when they were pupils in primary schools. The educational environment is too dynamic to gain significant benefit from the reproduction of past learning – culturally and contextually primary education has moved on. Teachers need to be constantly learning and responding positively and constructively to a range of influences – not simply how the pupils responded to the last lesson.

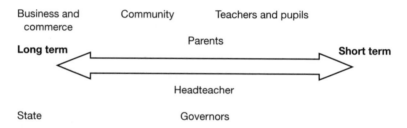

Figure 3.2 The continuum of stakeholders in education

The headteacher will need to exert an overarching influence on the school, from the policy and mission of the school as constructed with governors, to the daily focus on learning and teaching, working with the teaching staff and the pupils. Through that position they are best placed to act as a conduit for communication between the school and external bodies, such as the parents, the state and the local community. While the headteacher provides this central point of access to the school and outside bodies, the delegation of specific links to subject leaders is not just highly desirable but essential if the school is to operate efficiently.

Once an issue has been identified, for example the personal physical fitness of pupils, perhaps by parents or the PE subject leader, then the headteacher, possibly through the governors, may seek support through links with the local community. This may result in a local professional football team sending members of its youth squad to work with classes to help motivate the pupils into adopting a more positive approach to their personal fitness.

Concerns about the behaviour of children in the local community may be overcome through using the school as a means of bringing the concerned members of the community and the pupils together in a constructive way. This may be through the passing on of skills of local historical knowledge, with the children using the local community as an audience for their classroom output (their stories, art work, music) – getting to understand each other in a positive and constructive way.

Components of the curriculum

When all these influences on the construction of a curriculum for a primary school are taken into account, structurally it can be seen to have four distinct components. These will either be planned for or will be delivered through the culture of the school as part of a 'hidden' curriculum. If the school, and the subject leader, are aware of them they can be addressed much more successfully and coherently as the formal approach to learning in the school. Dryden and Vos (2001: 453) place them in this specific order:

1 personal-growth curriculum;
2 life-skills curriculum;
3 learning-to-learn, learning-to-think curriculum; and
4 content curriculum.

They argue that unless pupils develop appropriate self-confidence, are well motivated (and self-motivated) and have the necessary skills to communicate and relate positively to others they will not be 'turned on' to learning, making all other efforts largely irrelevant. By focusing upon developing an enthusiasm for learning through improving self-esteem, pupils will be in a much more positive emotional state.

Basic skills which will enable pupils to manage their lives confidently is the next level of the curriculum. This will include learning how to self-manage and work towards becoming an independent learner. This will involve developing problem identification and problem-solving skills, including conflict management strategies. Pupils will need to develop the skills necessary to access ICT, with the potential that has for further self-learning, along with elements of economics to enable them to manage their resources successfully.

The goal of developing as an independent learner can be realized as pupils are taught strategies for learning in such a way that they are able to apply them successfully across a range of contexts. Currently pupils tend to learn how to learn in a rather *ad hoc* way, through a combination of copying the models given to them by their teachers and parents and learning contextually dependent strategies (experimentation as science, text-based research as history). Only after these have been addressed does the content curriculum become a major focus for planning and learning. Even then, Dryden and Vos call for it to be constructed around integrated themes so that pupils are able to develop an appreciation of the interconnectedness of learning. In many respects this is precisely what the *Primary Strategy* (DfES, 2003) is calling for.

As a subject leader it is clearly important to work within the parameters and goals of the school, especially if something akin to the four-part curriculum underlies the educational thinking within the school. While the subject is a priority for the subject leader, it is subservient to the needs of the pupils and the educational goals of the school. The focus should be on examining where the learning derived from the subject can be used to enhance learning within the school for pupils as a whole.

Summary

The curriculum is a representation of the values and educational goals of the school. There are many factors which influence its construction and implementation but if it is to be effective it must have clarity of vision and purpose, an underlying philosophy and an approach that all stakeholders

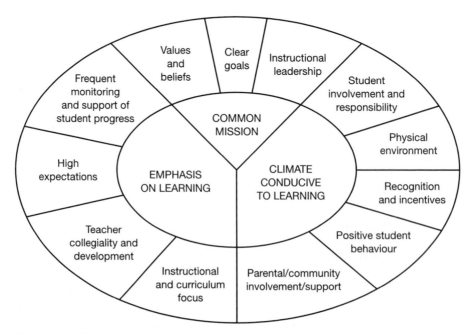

Figure 3.3 The parameters for an effective school
Source: Stoll and Fink (1996) *Changing Our Schools*. Buckingham: Open University Press. Reproduced with the kind permission of the Open University Press/McGraw-Hill Publishing Company.

can enthusiastically accept. Stoll and Fink's (1996) parameters for an effective school (Figure 3.3) encapsulate many of the factors discussed above. For the subject leader, the initial question is not what to teach but how. Once the classroom climate is established, the learning contexts can be more effectively delivered.

References

Alexander, R. (1988) 'Garden or jungle? Teacher development and informal primary education', in A. Blyth (ed.) *Informal Primary Education Today: Essays and Studies*. London: Falmer Press.

Burton, N. and Middlewood, D. (2001) 'Models of curriculum organisation', in D. Middlewood and N. Burton (eds) *Managing the Curriculum*. London: Paul Chapman Publishing.

DfE (Department for Education) (1995) *The National Curriculum*. London: HMSO.

DfEE (Department for Education and Employment) (1997) *Excellence in Schools*. London: HMSO.

DfES (Department for Education and Skills) (2003) *Excellence and Enjoyment – a Strategy for Primary Schools*. London: HMSO (online at http://www.dfes.gov.uk/primarydocument/).

DfES (Department for Education and Skills) (2004a) *The National Curriculum for England*. London: HMSO (online at http://www.nc.uk.net/index.html).

DfES (Department for Education and Skills) (2004b) *About the National Curriculum*. London: HMSO (online at http://www.nc.uk.net/nc_resources/html/valuesAimsPurposes.shtml.)

Dryden, G. and Vos, J. (2001) *The Learning Revolution*. Stafford: Network Educational Press.

Pollard, A. and Tann, S. (1987) *Reflective Teaching in the Primary School*. London: Cassell Education.

Preedy, P. (2000) 'Curriculum development with the Beacon Schools initiative', in M. Brundrett and N. Burton (eds) *The Beacon Schools Experience: Case Studies in Excellence*. Dereham: Peter Francis Publishers.

Reynolds, D. and Farrell, S. (1996) *Worlds Apart? A Review of International Surveys of Educational Achievement Involving England*. London: HMSO.

Silcock, P. and Brundrett, M. (2001) 'The management consequences of different models of teaching and learning', in D. Middlewood and N. Burton (eds) *Managing the Curriculum*. London: Paul Chapman Publishing.

Stoll, L. and Fink, D. (1996) *Changing our Schools*. Buckingham: Open University Press.

TTA (Teacher Training Agency) (1998) *National Standards for Subject Leaders*. London: TTA (online at http://www.tta.gov.uk/php/read.php?sectionid=103&articleid=519).

Vlaeminke, M. (1998) 'Historical and philosophical influences on the primary curriculum', in J. Moyles and L. Hargreaves (eds) *The Primary Curriculum: Learning from International Perspectives*. London: Routledge.

Wragg, E. (1997) *The Cubic Curriculum*. London: Routledge.

Recommended reading

Middlewood, D. and Burton, N. (2001) *Managing the Curriculum*, London: Paul Chapman.

Website

http://matrix.ncsl.org.uk

SECTION B

Establishing a Direction

4

Leadership, management and the middle leader

LEARNING OUTCOMES OF THIS CHAPTER

By the end of this chapter you should be able to:

- understand more about the nature of leadership and management and the inter-relationship between these terms
- articulate the phases of leadership and recognize the emerging role of the middle leader
- describe and analyse the importance of developing distributed leadership in primary schools

Defining leadership and management

The inter-related concepts of leadership and management contain a set of overlapping ideas that can lead to confusion about whether a particular function or activity in school fits into one category or the other. Indeed, we need to remember that these terms have been used differently at different times and in different places and there are even alternative phrases that are employed in other countries for the same activities. For instance, in the USA or Canada, it is quite common to hear the term 'educational administration' employed for many of the same activities that would be described as 'educational leadership' in the UK and it is important to be aware of this when reading texts written by authors from those countries (Coleman and Earley, 2005: 7). In general the chronology of the usage of the terms leadership and management is such that we should really refer to 'management then leadership' because the term management was far more ubiquitous as a description of the activities involved in running a school until the 1990s, when the use of the word 'leadership' really began to come into its own.

If we try to define the generally accepted differences between these terms we find that management tends to be seen as the kind of things that are more transactional in nature whereas leadership is seen as involving the longer term, the strategic and even the inspirational. A list of items that might be viewed as falling into one category or the other is shown in Table 4.1.

Table 4.1 Leadership as opposed to management

Leadership activities	Management activities
Creating a vision	Writing reports and other documents
Defining a mission	Chairing meetings
Encouraging and enabling staff to act as leaders in their own right	Monitoring the budget
Setting long-term objectives for a budget	Undertaking performance management reviews
Enhancing learning through developing new concepts of pedagogy	Observing teaching
	Timetabling or curriculum discussions
Working with parents and the wider community to create a sense of ownership and shared views	Organizing professional development activities
	Holding parents' evenings

There are clear differences between these two sets of activities but it is important to note that there are also very strong connections between the two. For instance, there would be little point in going to the trouble of creating a sense of vision and mission about a school unless this was written down and communicated to all parties. Indeed, although the creation of any real sense of direction for a school should involve as many stakeholders as possible, the actual act of writing may in itself be part of that process of formulating the vision. Jumping to the end of the list it is hard to think how a school leader would create a sense of ownership and shared views for parents and other stakeholders unless they were involved in activities like parents' evenings. So, in essence, leadership and management can be seen as being qualitatively different but they are fundamentally interconnected and it is true to say that schools need to be both led *and* managed. These days, however, it is the term leadership that has tended to be seen as the more important, as evidenced by the creation of various 'leadership programmes', many of which come under the remit of the National College for School Leadership that was set up in 2000 and moved into permanent buildings on a site next to the University of Nottingham in 2002. For this reason it is the concept of leadership that will form the focus of the rest of this chapter.

- What activities do you currently undertake that could be described as falling into the categories of 'leadership tasks' and 'management tasks'?
- How do the two sets of activities interconnect?
- What new leadership and management task might you take on that would enable you develop new skills as a leader in school?

The linguistic shift from the usage of 'management' to 'leadership' also symbolized a change in the way that schools are organized and it is no mere coincidence that this happened during a period when UK educational establishments were making an extraordinary journey of change from being regulated by local education authorities to being self-managing and autonomous units. Prior to the Education Act, 1988, school budgets were set centrally by local education authorities and headteachers and governors had financial control over comparatively small sums of money, usually termed 'capitation', used to purchase teaching materials. At this time leadership (if the term was used at all) was often seen as being vested in the hands of one person – the headteacher. The arrival of local financial management and the myriad of other initiatives that have characterized the period since the late 1980s have meant that leadership is now viewed in an entirely different way. It is now the prevailing view that leadership is a permeable process that is widely distributed throughout the school; indeed, many talk about it as an empowering process enabling others in the school, in their turn, to exercise leadership (Dimmock, 2003). Behind such notions is the rationale that a high-performing school can only be achieved if all staff are working together and taking on appropriate leadership functions and activities at their level in the organization. In some senses this is an indication that there are so many activities and initiatives occurring in schools at any one time that there is simply too much leadership required for this to be vested in the hands of one person.

For all these reasons leadership as a distributed concept is an increasingly influential notion that now underpins many national strategies for professional development and school improvement. For example, the National College for School Leadership (NCSL) has shown an increasing commitment to distributed leadership which led to the development of specific programmes such as 'Leading from the Middle', aimed at middle managers such as department heads and year co-ordinators. There is also a growing number of theoretical and empirical studies that explore both the theory and practice of distributed leadership, some of which suggest that such ideas can be extended to all staff and pupils within the school rather than being confined to professional educators such as teachers. Behind all this is a view of leadership as an influence process rather than a set of tasks associated with a particular position. In reality, leadership is both. It is an influence process and that is what makes it generic across levels of an organization. However, incumbents of different positions also need to apply the influence processes to particular spheres of responsibility within which there are specific tasks to be performed. For this reason programmme developers of in-service training courses will need to consider how the content of such programmes will differ between teacher, middle manager and senior leadership.

Phases of leadership

Scholars in the field of educational leadership have given relatively scant attention to developing theories of career progression in the profession. This is particularly the case for empirically supported theories. Recent interest has focused on identifying leadership stages and a number of schema have resulted. As Dimmock (2003) has pointed out, these originate, however, more from a conceptual than an empirical base. Consequently, this aspect of leadership remains a 'hot topic' for future empirical research. There is as yet no universally agreed, unequivocal consensus on a stage theory of leadership. The NCSL has published a five-stage model of career leadership as follows (NCSL, 2001). The first stage is recognized as 'emergent leadership', which is meant to apply to teachers who begin to take on management and leadership responsibilities and perhaps aspire to become headteachers. There is some equivocation here, because subject or specialist teachers are distinguished from emergent leaders and are regarded as 'middle' leaders. Clearly, the membership of both groups will overlap, even if the purpose of their tasks is ostensibly different. This duality is represented in the conceptual framework of middle leadership outlined in Chapter 1, and it is these groups that form the main audience for this text since they are the teachers who occupy the crucial ground between classroom teachers and the senior management team in many primary schools. A second stage of 'established leadership' comprises assistant and deputy heads, who are experienced leaders, but who do not intend to pursue headship. A third stage is recognized as 'entry to headship' and this stage combines the professional preparation for headship with the induction of new heads, a process seen as continuous and seamless. A fourth stage of 'advanced leadership' applies to mature leaders who are looking to refresh and update and widen their experience. Finally, a fifth stage, known as 'consultant leaders', are those who are sufficiently able and experienced to act in the capacity of trainer, mentor, inspector and to put something back into the profession.

The emerging role of the middle leader

The focus of leadership in schools is thus shifting from the headteacher towards a more participative view that encompasses participation in leadership from teachers (Day *et al.*, 1998; NCSL, 2001; Gold *et al.*, 2003). The aim should be that staff can pool their expertise and initiatives in a way that produces actions and benefits that are greater than those they could achieve alone (Gronn, 2002). Indeed, the plethora of policy initiatives that have impacted upon schools in recent years have created a situation where it is difficult to be a leader who takes sole responsibility and authority (Harris and Day, 2003). Dimmock (2003) argues that the thinking behind this is that high performance is associated with every area acting to support leadership. Nevertheless, Wright (2003) points out that collaborative models of leadership may ignore some of the tensions facing school leaders who have to negotiate a way forward in the light of Ofsted views about their effectiveness, performance tables and government programmes and advice.

In the light of these pressures it may not always be appropriate for schools to adopt such collaborative practices. While research by Riley and MacBeath (2003) indicates that a number of headteachers have developed collective practice through forward planning, self-development and staff development, some heads use key individuals among the staff to promote their own agenda. Moreover, Blasé and Blasé (1999) warn shared forms of governance may also allow leaders to control staff at a more subtle level. For example, having a select group of teachers making decisions can be another form of control, even if less visible because it creates a feeling of teacher involvement.

One factor that may actually mitigate against the development of middle leadership is the role of the headteacher as currently constituted in English schools because the head remains ultimately responsible for the school and thus maintains a considerable degree of authority over the rest of the staff. This is not to underplay the continuing role of the headteacher since they have an important role in directing school improvement through making crucial decisions about staff (Collins, 2001). The headteacher plays a key role in influencing middle management through a control over the distribution of responsibility, while subject leaders focus their leadership to a particular curriculum area without holding any line management responsibility for their colleagues (Fletcher-Campbell, 2003). What seems clear is that improving learning processes and outcomes entails collaboration and that decentralized and participatory leadership rather than top-down delegation is effective (Harris, 2003).

Such an emphasis on decentralized leadership informs the increasing focus on the role of subject leaders and classroom teachers in leading and managing schools and, in turn, raises issues about the training and development of such post-holders. Burns (2002: 55), at the time a director in the Innovation Unit in the DfES, has stated that: 'For the next phase of government reform to stand a real chance of success, there is no alternative but to invest in developing the capacity and status of the teaching profession.' This is a laudable aim that will require the systematic development of the contribution of teachers in making decisions about their future approaches to educating children, thereby encouraging a stance where teachers believe that their active involvement is important and valued. Giving teachers some 'ownership' and responsibility for the changes made within schools can only contribute to this view. Many teachers have been involved in contributing to school improvement through taking responsibility for leading a curriculum area throughout the school. Therefore they take ownership and enhance their expertise in a particular area of school development. Ribbins (2003) points out the issue of collegiality may be more complex than it at first seems and he goes on to argue that it is possible for teachers to feel involved in and contributors to change and development while working in a hierarchical structure where one person acts as a 'strong' leader. This works if the position of the leader is seen as justified through his or her abilities and knowledge.

If leadership is devolved, shared or distributed rather than being seen to be a capacity exercised by one individual in a hierarchy, then questions about the qualities of effective leadership come to the fore. Campbell and Southworth's (1992) study of cultures of collaboration found that individuals were valued as people, for their contribution to others and as part of a team. Greater openness was promoted and this was fostered by creating a secure environment. Leaders must therefore take account of the relationships between people, how interaction is developed within the school community and how individuals are enriched. West-Burnham (2002) speaks of the value of interpersonal intelligence in communicating honestly, sharing responsibility and interdependency; such intelligence is said to encourage tolerance, respect for others, self-esteem and understanding and is seen as a strong motivating factor. This notion is supported by the *Subject Leadership: Key Reference Handbook* (2002), which encourages teachers to respect all forms of intelligence and to make provision for all forms to be developed.

The words 'value' and 'trust' also appear with a notably regularity in publications about effective leadership. Bryk and Schneider (2002) found that trust has an impressive effect on school improvement and Bottery (2003) states that it is vital to have genuine two-way trust in order to create self-worth and job satisfaction. In order to encourage a culture of trust, sharing and learning, the leadership styles employed by all in schools become significant. Jeffrey and Woods (2003: 127) argue that collaboration must involve 'valuing individuals, interdependence, openness and trust', while Jones (2003) links feeling valued with distributed leadership and argues for devolution of responsibility wherever possible alongside working together as a team in order to make staff feel valued and empowered. It is equally clear that such devolution of power leads teachers to become involved, very healthily, in innovation and change (Atkins, 2002; Blaker, 2002; Walters, 2002). Values are also seen as important in terms of the moral stance taken by schools and, for Fullan (2001), this involves acting in an attempt to improve the lives of those within and external to the organization. Thus leadership is, at least in part, about the underlying philosophies and rationales upon which education and school practice are based, and these values also have a bearing on the style of leadership preferred (Dimmock, 2003).

The key elements important to effective middle leadership highlighted within the literature might be summarized as follows (it is important to recognize that these characteristics also need to be true of school leaders in order for middle leaders to be effective). Effective middle leaders:

- should be enthusiastic and self-confident;
- need to share their expertise and knowledge;
- must listen to colleagues and value their opinions;
- will work with colleagues to develop a vision and strategies to realize that vision;
- should communicate honestly and build a culture of mutual trust and respect; and
- need to be clear about their educational values and philosophies. (Hammerley-Fletcher and Brundrett, 2005).

Headteachers and subject leaders talk favourably about models of leadership which involve all staff in collaborating on and discussing school development and many believe in delegated responsibilities where everyone has some opportunity to demonstrate leadership and to develop leadership skills. For headteachers this involves them in having the courage to share or hand over aspects of their responsibility to others. They must also be aware of the developmental needs of their staff and celebrate their achievements. For subject leaders this means taking on and developing their area of responsibility and working with others to utilize colleagues' expertise, experience and energy. Nevertheless, subject leaders also recognize that the extent to which they are given responsibility relies on the attitudes and philosophies of the head. They regard the head as the ultimate leader and this is seen as an acceptable expression of a necessary and appropriate hierarchy. Nonetheless, it is clear that the forms and models of leadership utilized need to vary over time and between people and their roles. Thus notions about emotional literacy may become important in deciding what leadership structures may be appropriate and when they should be implemented, changed or adjusted.

Case study

Kim has been the subject co-ordinator for maths in a primary school for four years. She was asked to undertake a project to develop a system of early intervention to counteract underachievement in her subject and carried out a nine-month project to develop the initiative in the school. Kim worked with the headteacher and a coach in the school in order to bring together a team of staff; she defined a clear vision for what she wanted to achieve and broke down the project into small steps. Kim planned ahead and developed an action plan that linked into the school development plan. An Ofsted inspection intervened in the middle of the project, which, at first, seemed to threaten her work but her team 'stuck together' and it was decided that the Ofsted inspection actually gave them the impetus to put their plans into action. The Ofsted inspection went very well and there were special compliments about maths in the school which included an acknowledgement that 'Mathematics is led very well with a clear vision'. This experience has enabled Kim to feel much more confident as a leader and she is now writing a programme for numeracy for a Key Stage 1 network based on the research she has undertaken for her previous project. After the initiative, Key Stage 1 meetings became 'a lot more enthusiastic' and she has gone on to work with the head with an aim to make the school an LEA Maths Centre.

Forms of distributed leadership

A study of 24 primary schools carried out by Hammersley-Fletcher and reported in Hammersley-Fletcher and Brundrett (2005) noted that two aspects, forms or types of distributed leadership appeared in the schools:

1 Those where distributed leadership was being discussed and talked about, but the subject leaders were limited to implementing the strategies of others. Headteachers could be relied upon and were 'leading from the front'. This results in some thinking about leadership, but restricts freedom to create new strategies.
2 Those where there was active distributed leadership, where creative and original ideas are both facilitated and expected through the leadership system. In these schools subject leaders are able to implement research-based ideas in a no-blame culture, where children and vision are seen as paramount. The headteacher facilitates such innovation, rather than directs it.

Hammersley-Fletcher and Brundrett suggest that, in order to enact and ensure distributed leadership really comes into existence, schools need some method in place to force staff 'out of their nest'. Staff need to be put into positions of true leadership, where creativity and innovation were expected, varied from school to school but where this happened it developed knowledge and support, which resulted in greater confidence. Such innovations take a substantial amount of confidence on the part of the headteacher to encourage a capacity for learning in his or her staff and systems to encourage a culture of self-development need to be in place before the headteacher can step back from the 'front line.' However the reward for such developments is a confident and self-improving school. Schools thus have a number of priorities which will include: developing the subject leader's strategic leadership skills; improving his or her mediation and interpersonal skills; opening up greater possibilities for motivating colleagues; and the need to support a learning environment through realistic and incremental developments.

There are resource implications to the kind of developments enumerated above. Middle leaders will need training, development and, above all, time to take on the new roles that are increasingly expected of them. There are signs that a commitment exists to provide this resource in the form of national training initiatives such as 'Leading from the Middle' and changes to the pattern of work embodied in the Workforce Remodelling Agreement that will be discussed in detail in Chapter 10. Large questions remain as to whether the resource will be sufficient to meet the need.

Summary

Schools have been subjected to multiple and complex change in recent years and there is a strong argument for increased stability in the system. nonetheless, change is an ever-present factor in life and public institutions are not immune from the forces that impact on society as a whole. The increasingly globalized nature of society, the impact of ICT, new discoveries in learning theory and the concept of local leadership and management have all, from the macro to the micro level, ensured that schools need to have robust measures in place to adapt rapidly. The sheer volume and pace of innovation have meant that traditional, hierarchical forms of leadership in schools, which focus power, authority and responsibility in the hands of the headteacher, have to be supplanted or at the very least modified in order to create the leadership capacity that is required. Inevitably this has both empowered and challenged middle leaders in schools. New notions of distributed leadership hold out the possibility of a more inclusive, more adaptive approach, to school leadership but the concept of distributed leadership is itself more of an aspiration that an actuality in many schools. Headteachers, governing bodies, local and national government organizations must work together to ensure that middle leaders are developed, trained, empowered and resourced to take on new and complex roles that will benefit outcomes for pupils.

References

Atkins, J. (2002) 'Providing space for innovation and autonomy', *Education Review*, 16: 14–19.

Bell, D. and Ritchie, R. (1999) *Towards Effective Subject Leadership in the Primary School*. Buckingham: Open University Press.

Blaker, G. (2002) 'From staffroom to innovation strategy room – can it be done?', *Education Review*, 16: 76–85.

Blasé, J. and Blasé, J. (1999) 'Implementation of shared governance for instructional improvement; principals' perspectives', *Journal of Educational Administration*, 37: 476–500.

Bottery, M. (2003) 'The leadership of learning communities in a culture of unhappiness', *School Leadership and Management*, 23: 187–207.

Bryk, A. and Schneider, B. (2002) *Trust in Schools*. New York, NY: Russell Sage.

Burns, M. (2002) 'Making innovation stick', *Education Review Innovation and Autonomy*, 16: 51–5.

Campbell, P. and Southworth, G. (1992) 'Rethinking collegiality: teachers' views', in N. Bennett *et al.* (eds) *Managing Change in Education.* Buckingham: Open University Press.

Coleman, M. and Earley, P. (2005) *Theories and Practice of Leadership: An Introduction.* Oxford: Oxford University Press.

Collins, J. (2001) *Good to Great.* New York, NY: HarperCollins.

Day, C., Hall, C. and Whitaker, P. (1998) *Developing Leadership in Primary Schools.* London: Paul Chapman Publishing.

Dimmock, C. (2003) 'Leadership in learning-centred schools: cultural context, functions and qualities', in M. Brundrett *et al.* (eds) *Leadership in Education.* London: Sage.

Fletcher-Campbell, F. (2003) 'Promotion to middle management: some practitioners' perceptions', *Educational Research,* 45: 1–15.

Fullan, M. (2001) *Leading in a Culture of Change.* San Francisco, CA: Jossey-Bass.

Glatter, R. (2003) 'Which path to reform', *Education Journal,* 69: 10.

Gold, A., Evans, J., Earley, P., Halpin, D. and Collarbone, P. (2003) 'Principled principals? Values-driven leadership: evidence from ten case studies of "outstanding" school leaders', *Educational Management and Adminsitration,* 31: 127–38.

Gronn, P. (2002) 'Distributed leadership', in K. Leithwood *et al.* (eds) *Second International Handbook of Educational Leadership and Administration.* Dordrecht: Kluwer.

Hammersley-Fletcher, L. and Brundrett, M. (2005) 'Leaders on leadership: the thoughts of primary school headteachers and subject leaders', *School Leadership and Management,* 25: 59–76.

Harris, A. (2003) 'Introduction: challenging the orthodoxy of school leadership: towards alternative theoretical perspectives', *School Leadership and Management,* 23: 125–8.

Harris, A. and Day, C. (2003) 'From singular to plural? Challenging the orthodoxy of school leadership', in N. Bennett and L. Anderson (eds) *Rethinking Educational Leadership.* London: Sage.

Jeffrey, B. and Woods, P. (2003) *The Creative School: A Framework for Success, Quality and Effectiveness.* London: RoutledgeFalmer.

Jones, M. (2003) 'What makes a good school?', *New Era in Education,* 84.

National College for School Leadership (2001) *Leadership Development Framework.* Nottingham: NCSL: 37–8.

Ribbins, P. (2003) 'A life in design: a school subject leader's story.' Keynote paper presented at the BELMAS national conference, Milton Keynes, October.

Riley, K. and MacBeath, J. (2003) 'Effective Leaders and Effective Schools', in N. Bennett, M. Crawford and C. Riches (eds) *Managing Change in Education*. Buckingham: Open University: 101–18.

West-Burnham, J. (2002) *The Emotionally Intelligent School. NCSL Thinkpiece*. Nottingham: NCSL.

Wright, N. (2003) 'Principled or "bastard" leadership? A rejoinder to Gold, Evans, Earley, Halpin and Collarbone', *Educational Management and Adminsitration*, 31: 139–43.

Recommended reading

Brundrett, M. (ed.) (1999) *Principles of School Leadership*. King's Lynn: Peter Francis Publishing.

Brundrett, M. (2000) *Beyond Competence: The Challenge for Educational Management*. King's Lynn: Peter Francis Publishing.

Brundrett, M., Burton, N. and Smith, R. (eds) (2002) *Leadership in Education*. London: Sage.

Bush, T. and Bell, L. (2002) *The Principles and Practice of Educational Management*. London: Paul Chapman Publishing.

Earley, P. and Weindling, D. (2004) *Understanding School Leadership*. London: Paul Chapman Publishing.

Websites

British Educational Leadership, Management and Administration Society (http://www.shu.ac.uk/belmas).

DfES A–Z of School Leadership and Management (http://www.dfes.gov.uk/a-z/atozindex_ba.html).

National College for School Leadership (http://www.ncsl.org.uk).

5

Middle leaders managing change

LEARNING OUTCOMES OF THIS CHAPTER

By the end of this chapter you should be able to:

- understand more about the nature of change, especially in the context of schools
- recognize the key notions connected with working within a development or improvement plan
- distinguish between action-planning and target-setting and be able to reflect on their importance in school development and improvement

Change: the one constant

In the broad historical sweep of cultural development it is one of the greatest of ironies that the tendency for systems to change has been seen as one of the few constants. Such notions predate our modern concerns and the acceptance of mutability can be observed in the philosophical tradition dating back to the Ancient Greeks. Nonetheless, there is a consensus that certain eras witness dramatic shifts in technological development and intellectual innovation, such as the industrial revolution of the eighteenth and nineteenth centuries, which cause particularly dramatic periods of change. The late twentieth century and early twenty-first centuries appear to have been another such period since there has been rapid development in the scientific, technological and social spheres that has altered the landscape of the leadership, management and governance of education and other socially codified institutions. In an influential and persuasive series of texts, Fullan (1993; 1999; 2003) has argued that the increasingly diverse nature of societies, the revolution in communications technologies and new attitudes to learning have ensured that complexity and change are an unavoidable part of life in schools.

The stages in the change process are seen as initiation, implementation, continuation and outcome (Fullan, 2001) but such conceptions provide a dangerously rationalistic formulation that can make innovation seem simple, linear and value free. In this sense the recent fascination with school development planning and strategic management in schools can be seen as an attempt to insert a rational model on to the frequently disordered and fluctuating circumstances that schools find themselves in (Morrison, 1998: 13). Nonetheless, while accepting Mintzberg's (1987) famous formulation, that we should accept an emergent approach that views change as a continuous, open-ended and largely unpredictable process, this chapter will outline the importance of a strategic approach to change which attempts to provide a mapping process that will lead the organization forward.

We must also remember that change may be inevitable but both what we change and the way we change must but governed by a moral imperative that examines both our commitment to pupils' learning and staff relationships. It has also become a truism in education that we are good at the first stages of the change cycle, that of initiating change, but we are far less successful as seeing it through. There are great dangers here because the process of inducing change can be challenging, difficult and even painful. If such change does not lead to sustained improvement that helps pupils and staff, the innovation has not only failed in its targets and goals but it has also caused a great deal of distress for no reason. As Everard et al. (2004: 285–6) point out, the last thing that we want is a façade of change followed by a gradual sinking back into old ways of working. Indeed the best models of change integrate these issues of complexity, moral purpose and the need for sustained and embedded improvement by suggesting that organizational change in schools is based on a number of key factors that echo throughout this text and include engagement of parents and community resources; access to new ideas; professional community; internalizing responsibility for change; and strategic educational planning (Bryk et al., cited in Fullan, 1999: 35).

Within many formulations of the ways in which schools can be encouraged to cope with such complexity the headteacher has been seen as the main change agent but it has been realized for some time that the distribution of power and authority within a school is a crucial aspect of the change process (Dalin, 1998) and, in particular, the success or failure of curriculum innovation is contingent upon the commitment and professional development of teachers (Blenkin et al., 1997). Individualism and collectivism must have equal power and every person is a change agent (Fullan, 1993). This realization places middle leaders at the heart of school development – either as substantial roadblocks or as invaluable facilitators or innovators. As this chapter progresses to discuss strategy, improvement planning and target-setting, while we do not suggest that middle leaders can take ownership of the overall visualization and construction of such policies, we do wish to suggest that they have what is both figuratively and quite literally a central role to play in school development and improvement.

Case study

Helen has been a Key Stage 1 maths and ICT co-ordinator in her present school for three years. One of the priorities on the school development plan was to improve differentiation in planning and make it more evident in children's work. Helen worked with the headteacher and coach in the school. She felt that it was important to communicate her vision and enthusiasm and to inspire her colleagues and she was keen to encourage references to the National Numeracy Strategy and QCA ICT units. All teaching staff contributed to staff meetings on differentiation, a whole-school definition was agreed on and success criteria for the project were agreed. Helen brought together a team of staff and worked hard to motivate and enthuse the group by keeping them informed of developments. She was careful to make her colleagues feel valued and encouraged their contributions in staff meetings. She went out of her way to show that she did not have fixed ideas about the project but was open to change based on their suggestions. Helen was careful to check that staff understood what was being asked of them by working with them in a relaxed atmosphere where developments and amendments could be made in way that was not threatening to their professionalism. When colleagues expressed concerns over the workload implications of the initiative Helen took these seriously and confirmed that the new planning sheets that were proposed were merely a beneficial extension of their current practice, as modelled by Helen's own examples. Staff in the school are now differentiating effectively in ICT and maths lessons and evidence of differentiation in lesson plans and children's work has been collected. There is now an agreed whole-school approach to maths and ICT and differentiation is established as part of day-to-day practice.

Contributing to a school's strategy and working within a development or improvement plan

Strategy is a difficult concept to pin down and its use can be especially difficult to define in the context of schools. The origins of the word lie in military values, which is the reason why it is a challenging term to employ in the social context of educational settings. As a general working definition is can be seen as 'the broad overall direction that an organization wishes to move in' (Fidler, 2002: 9). In this sense strategy can been as the *big picture* or the *long-term set of goals* for a school. As with the rest of leadership and management such strategy has tended to be seen as the responsibility of the headteacher and governing body who decide on the broad objectives of the school which will then be enacted by the rest of the staff. As the new ideas of distributed leadership have begun to take hold this older monolithic view has increasingly begun to break down and it is increasingly accepted that all members of staff, and indeed all stakeholders, should be involved in developing the strategy for a school. There are essentially two reasons for this that relate to the nature of the decision-making process and efficacy of any plan that may emerge. Schools are complex organizations that involve the aspirations of pupils, parents, staff and a wider community that links into local and national government. It is also important to remember that many schools remain closely aligned to religious denominations that may have paid for their foundation and may contribute to their continued upkeep. The involvement of as many stakeholders as possible helps to ensure that the goals set for a school reflect the views of the different stakeholder groups that the school encompasses. Such involvement also offers and opportunity for decisions to be legitimized through a process of discussion and scrutiny from as many internal external partners as possible. We must also remember that any good strategy 'involves the whole organization in a holistic way' (Fidler, 2002: 9) and so, quite simply, if a strategy is to be effective, then it must encourage the involvement of as many people as possible so that they have a sense of ownership and will want to take the strategy forward rather than fighting against it or ignoring its most salient points. Fidler (2002: 10) argues that strategy takes account of the following:

- Long-term intentions and aspirations.
- The external environment (both now and future predictions).
- The internal strengths of an organization.
- The prevailing organizational culture.
- Expectations of stakeholders.
- Likely future resources.

All these actions or issues are underpinned by the values and vision of the organization that defined the strategy which will inform operational planning. Davies and Davies (2005: 12) suggest that the moral purpose and values of an organization must combine with the vision and futures perspective of a school in order to create the circumstances where a strategy can emerge. This strategy will, in turn, define the operational planning and current, real-time, actions and reactions of the staff.

Target-setting and action-planning

Overall long-term strategy will indicate the future direction of a school but such futures planning will need to be focused down into a timetable of actions that can begin to make the day-to-day differences in a school that will lead to improvement. Fidler (2002: 11) suggests that planning timescales work at different but inter-related levels, as shown in Table 5.1.

Table 5.1 Planning timescales

Timescale	Key issues	Nature of objectives
The very long term	What will life be like in the future? What should schools be like?	Broad brush – long-term visioning
Long term	What are desirable developments?	Broad brush – overall aims of the school related to stakeholder groups. May include major aspirations for building developments and teaching and learning
Middle term	What are feasible developments?	Clearer – focusing down – may include medium-term financial goals
Medium term	Five-year plans	Clearer – may include spending plans for major refurbishments, staffing goals, major curriculum innovations
Short term	School development plans	Precise and clearly articulated objectives – may include annual spending goals, curriculum planning, staffing and financial targets

Source: After Fidler (2002: 11).

It has been argued that strategy development can be seen as a 'conveyor belt with short term plans working their way through and then dropping off the end of priorities or translating themselves into the completion of one element of longer term planning' (Fidler, 2002: 11). This is, however, something of a mechanistic approach to strategic leadership and we should remember that priorities change so swiftly in education that it can be difficult to maintain a consistent 'straight line' approach to strategy and planning. The key issue for leaders, especially at the curriculum level, is to translate strategy into actions because it is most commonly the curriculum leader who will address the short to medium-term issues that have direct impact on the lives of both staff and pupils. Davies and Davies (2005: 13) suggest a four-stage 'ABCD' approach to translating strategy into action, as shown in Table 5.2.

Table 5.2 The ABCD approach of translating strategy into action

	Stage	Elements
1	Articulate	Strategy
2	Build	Images Metaphors Experience
3	Create	Dialogues – conversations Cognitive/mental map Shared understanding
4	Define	Strategic perspective Outcome orientation Formal plans

Source: Davies and Davies (2005: 204).

The attractiveness of the ABCD approach comes from the fact that it incorporates the idea that strategy development is not necessarily a linear activity and it reveals that the best actions come after a clear articulation of the values of the organization allied to ongoing conversations between leaders and the led. For these reasons, Davies and Davies (2005: 14) argue persuasively that it is vital to build a common understanding of what is possible through shared experiences and images. This process of discussion is as important for subject leaders who are in charge of planning for action as it is for school senior managers who oversee long-term strategic developments. This involvement of staff serves a number of purposes (Busher *et al.*,

2000: 160). First it helps staff to feel involved and empowered and allows them to feel that they have a real role in evaluating their own practices and developing new ways of working. Secondly, in counterbalance, it lessens the chance that colleagues will see the planning process as a method of control that will deprive them of ownership of their work. Thirdly, it helps to promote staff development by engaging staff in a variety of activities. Overall this sense of involvement will encourage a collegial approach to working that makes staff feel as though they are involved in a shared set of activities that define and create the future together. This has a particular kind of importance for the curriculum leader who may be tasked with developing an action plan that will circumscribe the activities and duties of staff who are senior in the school hierarchy, or merely senior in years and experience.

Effective planning can be seen as being based on five interlocking processes:

1 Working with staff.
2 Establishing baselines: measuring current performance.
3 Having a clear vision of where to go.
4 Creating sensible maps, timetables and ladders to achieve the preferred goals.
5 Creating a means of monitoring progress on the road to achieving the goals (target-setting) (Busher *et al.*, 2000: 160).

These processes are very similar to those that need to be carried out by the headteacher when developing the overall strategy for the school. This is entirely right and proper since the key elements of school improvement apply at all levels in schools. The main differences that a curriculum co-ordinator may experience are, quite simply, in the number of people he or she will be working with and the limits on the topics that he or she will need to explore and discuss. Whereas the headteacher will need to have a 'helicopter view' that enables him or her to hover above the day-to-day management activities in order to see what issues are approaching on the horizon and so that he or she can map out the way he or she wishes the whole school to progress, the curriculum leader will necessarily focus on the subject area that he or she has in his or her charge. This will also require some degree observation and mapping of future direction but this will be limited to the subject at hand. Having stated this, however, it is important to remember that few subjects really stand alone in the wider curriculum since there may be important links to be developed or enhanced with other subjects, and leadership and management of the curriculum will also, necessarily, involve analysing staffing and resource needs in the present and future.

◆ What are the key current issues for your subject or class group at the moment?

◆ What new priorities do you see developing in the horizon that may relate to the school's overall mission, the needs of the children in your care or the changing national agenda?

The idea of setting targets to enhance achievement and overall outcomes has come to the fore in recent years and the national agenda has integrated such ideas in their recommendations to schools (see, for instance, DfEE, 1996). There is an element of top-down prescriptiveness in this development which grates on the sensibilities of some educators who are concerned that such target-setting tends to focus on a few measurable outcomes such as SATs results or other externally mandated features of school life. There is a great deal of truth in this and we must remember that we should attempt to measure what we value rather than value what we measure in education. Nonetheless, targets can be a powerful way of moving things forward in a school. Great emphasis has been placed on the importance of discussion and agreement building in this chapter, but transforming words into action can be problematic and the temptation to continue to talk indefinitely can be especially problematic in schools where a whole host of values, beliefs, and ethical and personal considerations can impact on the decision-making process.

The planning and development cycle

As Brundrett and Terrell (2004) point out, the key point to keep in mind about this process is that it should not simply be a bureaucratic exercise. If it is managed well it is a means of ensuring that the actual process of accountability is systematized and ordered – an issue that will be analysed further in Chapter 7. Development planning is now well established in many schools and subject leaders, as the school's middle managers, have a pivotal role to play in its construction and implementation. The key to its success is the extent to which it provides a clear sense of direction which everyone in the subject and senior management team can follow and understand. As we have seen, planning at the level of the subject or department means thinking about long-term and short-term issues and goals. The standard structure and organization for what has become known as the planning cycle involves the following key stages: *audit, vision, construction, implementation* and *evaluation*. This cyclical process helps to provide subject leaders with answers to several important questions which Fleming and Amesbury (2001: 120) have developed:

- Where are we now? (*audit*)
- Where do we want the developing subject/department to be in five years time? (*vision*)
- What changes do we need to make? (*construction*)
- How shall we manage these changes? (*implementation*)
- How shall we know whether our management of change has been successful? (*evalutation*)

The broad outline of this process normally follows the six-stage pattern set out below:

- Audit.
- Strategic plan.
- Subject development plan.
- Improvement plan.
- Key stage, year, subject and programme plans.
- Action plans (adapted from Fleming and Amesbury, 2001).

This cycle has close associations with the school improvement model that is outlined below and with the action research model that will be analysed in the last chapter of this book. The key notion here is the progressive and systematic movement from the big picture to the small but key and localized targets that make the individual improvements that lead to enhanced effectiveness overall.

From action-planning to target-setting

Targets are seen as an essential part of the British government's commitment to raising educational standards since they are seen as providing a clear focus for improvements, particularly in teaching and learning. It is argued that, at *primary* level, the implementation of the National Literacy and Numeracy Strategies, supported by the target-setting and wider accountability framework, brought about a substantial rise in standards (DfES, 2004: 2). The DfES *Guidance for LEAs on Target-setting at Key Stages 2, 3 and 4 and for School Attendance* (2004: 2) outlines a number of key principles for school performance targets and suggests that *school* targets should be:

- based on the prior attainment and expected progress of individual children in each cohort;
- ambitious;
- focused on equity as well as excellence; and
- owned.

The notion of benchmarked and ambitious targets accords with the thrust of all the policy on targets in recent years but the focus on equity and ownership is an interesting and new emphasis. The desire for equity came about because improvements in pupil attainment had not been spread evenly across all groups of pupils. This marks an acceptance of the notion that has been prevalent in school effectiveness and improvement circles that in-school differences may actually be more significant than between-school differences. The concept of ownership reflects much of the recent thrust on schools as learning organizations and may be one further indicator of a national acceptance of recent theories of distributed leadership and management. It is notable that this should be 'A whole-school approach to target-setting, which involves not just Head teachers and leadership teams, but also class teachers and, where appropriate teaching assistants, will ensure that the process is fully informed and rigorous' (DfES, 2004: 3). This inclusion of teaching assistants no doubt indicates the complex and challenging focus on workforce remodelling.

The DfEE (2001) document, *Supporting the Target Setting Process*, suggests that schools should adopt a policy of target-setting within a cycle of school self-improvement as part of a systematic approach to raising standards of pupil achievement. It is suggested that in most schools, key stages and expected National Curriculum levels are suitable timescales and measures for use in setting such targets – although these timelines may need to be amended for pupils with special needs: 'Targeting for improvement in this way serves as a focus for action planning, and as a basis for defining success criteria when monitoring and evaluating the effectiveness of the actions that the school has implemented' (DfEE, 2001: 6). The document suggests a five-stage cycle of self-improvement, as represented in Figure 5.1. Although the diagrammatic representation of the cycle reveals that this is a holistic and interconnected process the progression of the cycle can be identified according to five 'steps' outlined below.

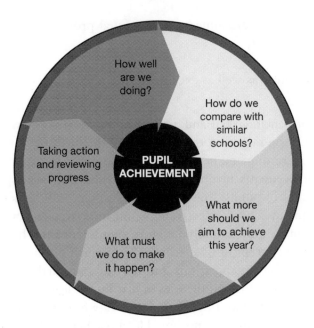

Figure 5.1 A five-stage cycle for school self-improvement
Source: DfEE (2001)
Crown copyright material is reproduced with the permission of the Controller of HMSO and the Queen's Printer for Scotland.

Step 1: How well are we doing?

Teachers assess what pupils have achieved in relation to the curriculum taught, where possible and appropriate, benchmarked against other, similar groups of pupils from within the school, either in the past or present. In most schools, National Curriculum level descriptions set the standards to use in English, mathematics and science, and pupils' performances at the end of a key stage are appropriate as measures of the school's overall performance. Schools may also consider some pupils' achievements in terms of their acquisition of independence skills based on judgements about the frequency of teacher interventions necessary during their learning. The challenge for schools is to identify the kinds of performance information that are available to show what their pupils are achieving and about which such questions can be asked. For those schools it may be important first to take stock of how pupils' performance is assessed throughout the school and to consider the school's assessment criteria, data collection systems and record-keeping (DfEE, 2001: 7).

Step 2: How do we compare with similar schools?

Teachers consider how well the school is doing, shown by its pupils' achievements, in the wider context of the performances achieved by similar pupils in other schools. Local and national benchmark information should enable like-for-like comparisons to be made. The performance criterion used in the national benchmark information is the proportion of pupils achieving the expected National Curriculum level, or better, at the end of Key Stages 1, 2 and 3, and GCSE grades and GCSE/GNVQ points scores at the end of Key Stage 4. This information may stimulate key questions such as: 'how do those better performing schools achieve what they do?' and 'what can we learn from those schools to raise the standards of achievement of our own pupils?' (DfEE, 2001: 9).

Step 3: What more should we aim to achieve this year?

Targets are set to drive school improvement and provide impetus and challenge complacency. Statutory targets apply to all schools, but schools can set additional targets that reflect relevant priorities. These additional targets can also be published alongside statutory targets in the school's annual governors' report to parents (DfEE, 2001: 12). To be effective, targets for school improvement, statutory or otherwise, need to be **SMART** targets. This means they should be **S**pecific, **M**easurable, **A**chievable and **R**ealistic, and set against an appropriate **T**imescale. SMART targets will be measurable and reflect the criteria used for measuring pupil performance. Teachers make judgements about translating practice into gains in pupils' performances in the future by deciding what more pupils will achieve when more successful teaching practices are implemented, over and above what they would be expected to achieve given current teaching practice. Those outcomes are the school's measurable targets (DfEE, 2001: 13).

Steps 4 and 5: Taking action

Having analysed the school's performance and set targets for school improvement, schools move from reviewing performance to taking action. Thus the shared and agreed picture of the school's performance and clear targets for improvement turn to action-planning. Action plans identify what is needed to achieve the targets, including the important changes that need implementing and how the action plan is to be supported with resources and staff development. Taking action may involve 'process targets', such as improving accommodation or integration opportunities which will contribute to the school's ability to meet its performance targets. It is important to put in place effective strategies to monitor and evaluate gains in pupils' performance as the new teaching practices take effect (DfEE, 2001: 17).

Such target-setting is increasingly informed by the use of national data that are increasingly accessible to senior managers and teachers. For instance, the target-setting tool in the Pupil Achievement Tracker (PAT) is intended to make it easier for schools to identify areas where pupils' progress is slower than that achieved nationally in high-performing similar schools. Teachers can use it to ask questions about the effectiveness of their classroom practice looking at graphical data on the progress made by their pupils; set pupil targets informed by the progress made by similar pupils nationally; and understand fully what pupils can achieve by the diagnostic analysis of test papers. Headteachers and senior managers can view recent performance against other similar schools to help set development priorities; ask questions about the achievement of different groups within the school; and review the success of different initiatives, particularly through the ability to group pupils and look at their achievement and progress.

Summary

The landscape of school life has changed so much in recent years that it is hard, if not impossible, for any one person to undertake all the leadership functions that are required. Not only this but the very notion of one person dominating the way in which a school should develop is increasingly seen as unacceptable. So headteachers have both practical and ethical reasons for ensuring that leadership and management activities are distributed throughout the organization. This distribution presents new challenges in turn for staff who will need to think beyond the confines of their own classrooms in order to take on responsibilities for whole-school developments even if such supervision is confined to one curriculum area of management function. Whatever level the leadership function is located and whoever is required to lead, the key issues in terms of planning are the same. The skilled leader, whether he or she is the headteacher or a newly qualified member of staff experiencing his or her first leadership activity, must take account of the aspirations of the wider community that he or she is serving, envision a future that improves school life for staff and pupils, and then help to create a new reality through discussion, careful planning and implementation.

References

Blenkin, G., Edwards, G. and Kelly, A. (1997) 'Perspectives on educational culture', in A. Harris *et al.* (eds) *Organizational Effectiveness and Improvement in Education*. Buckingham: Open University Press.

Brundrett, M. and Terrell, I. (eds) (2004) *Learning to Lead in the Secondary School: Becoming and Effective Head of Department*. London: RoutledgeFalmer.

Busher, H., Harris, A. and Wise, C. (2000) *Subject Leadership and School Improvement*. London: Paul Chapman Publishing.

Dalin, P. (1998) *School Development Theories and Strategies*. London: Cassell.

Davies, B. and Davies, B. (2005) 'Strategic leadership', in B. Davies (ed.) *The Essentials of School Leadership*. London: Paul Chapman Publishing.

Davies, B. and Ellison, L. (2003) *The New Strategic Direction and Development of the School* (2nd edn). London: RoutledgeFalmer.

DfEE (1996) *Setting Targets to Raise Standards*. London: HMSO.

DfEE (1998) *Circular 11/98: Target Setting in Schools*. London: DfEE.

DfEE (2001) *Supporting the Target Setting Process*. London: DfEE (online at http://www.standards.dfes.gov.uk/ts/pdf/DfES_065_2001.pdf).

DfES (2004) *Guidance for LEAs on Target-setting at Key Stages 2, 3 and 4 and for School Attendance* (online at http://www.standards.dfes.gov.uk/ts/rtf/targetguidance2004.rtf).

Everard, K.B., Morris, G. and Wilson, I. (2004) *Effective School Management* (4th edn). London: Paul Chapman Publishing.

Fidler, B. (2002) *Strategic Management for School Development: Leading your School's Improvement Strategy*. London: British Educational Leadership, Management and Administration Society/Paul Chapman Publishing.

Fleming, P. and Amesbury, M. (2001) *The Art of Middle Management in Primary Schools*. London: David Fulton.

Fullan, M. (1993) *Change Forces: Probing the Depths of Educational Reform*. London: Falmer Press.

Fullan, M. (1999) *Change Forces: The Sequel*. London: Falmer Press.

Fullan, M. (2001) *The New Meaning of Educational Change*. London: RoutledgeFalmer.

Fullan, M. (2003) *Change Forces with a Vengeance*. London: RoutledgeFalmer.

Mintzberg, H. (1987) 'Crafting strategy', *Harvard Business Review*, March/April: 66–75.

Morrison, K. (1998) *Management Theories for Educational Change*. London: Paul Chapman Publishing.

Recommended reading

Davies, B. (ed.) (2005) *The Essentials of School Leadership*. London: Paul Chapman Publishing.

Fidler, B. (1996) *Strategic Planning for School Improvement*. London: Financial Times/Pitman Publishing.

Hargreaves, D.H. and Hopkins, D. (1994) *Development Planning for School Improvement*. London: Cassell.

Websites

DfES (2001) *Supporting the Target Setting Process* (http://www.standards. dfes.gov.uk/ts/pdf/DfES_065_2001.pdf). Further information on target-setting, including case studies, is also available on the DfES's website at www.standards.dfes.gov.uk/ts/.

For information on the School and College Achievement and Attainment Tables (formerly Performance Tables) see http://dfes.gov.uk/performancetables/.

Information on the Pupil Achievement Tracker, see http://www.standards. dfes.gov.uk/performance/pat/.

6

Monitoring and evaluating progress

LEARNING OUTCOMES OF THIS CHAPTER

By the end of this chapter you should be able to:

- recognize the importance of monitoring progress
- understand the key indicators of progress
- articulate the key issues in effective monitoring

'Getting there': monitoring progress

The preceding three chapters have focused on locating the school in terms of its current position relative to expectations, setting appropriate targets for improvement based upon the potential of staff and pupils and identifying potential strategies for successfully achieving those targets. Ultimately this chapter will address two key questions within the change process:

1 Are we getting there?
2 Are we there yet?

In the previous chapter the importance of targets was emphasized – they provide an all-important sense of direction because, if you don't know where you are going, then anywhere will do. Monitoring is the process by which the journey towards those targets can be tracked and checked against expectations of progress. It can provide encouragement that reassures the school that they are making appropriate progress in the right direction. It can also provide an early-warning of progress being behind schedule or moving off focus. To do this monitoring has to keep a clear view of both the original position and the position that is being moved towards, to ensure that movement is towards the latter and away from the former. Evaluation checks the current position, usually at a point when it is perceived that the targets have been met, or the time by which they were to have been achieved has expired, against the expected target position. It also provides an opportunity to look back on the route that was taken and to consider the implications for future, similar journeys. The taxonomy employed by Stake (1976) implies that monitoring is a formative process and evaluation is summative.

Indicators of progress

In attempting to identify and define the more 'educationally desirable' position that the school wishes to find itself in as a result of a process of change, a school may need to resort to defining outcome in more quantifiable terms. The goal of improving the quality of mathematics teaching across the school through approaches which encourage a greater enjoyment of the subject from children and, as a result, more effective learning, may be reduced to a target concerning the results from maths tests. It would be all too easy for the maths tests to become the entire focus of the improvement effort. Rather than being a target, the tests should be regarded as an indicator of the effectiveness of the 'good practice' that has been the focus of the change – it is the process that is the important element here as it offers a long-term solution to ensuring a deeper level of learning on the part of the pupils. It is analogous to the classroom situation whereby the use of a worksheet to provide evidence of learning can become corrupted if the teaching effort is misdirected to ensuring the correct completion of the worksheet rather than the learning which will enable it to be completed correctly. The former is a superficial approach which may be easier to achieve but will have less of a long-term impact than the latter approach.

The identification of appropriate indicators is important and useful in terms of gauging progress and measuring relative success. They are not the targets that are being worked towards, they are far too superficial for that, but they are important externally because oversimplistic targets are often used as a means of judging success without adequate regard to how those targets are achieved. By all means identify targets which will make it easy to judge the relative success of an improvement, but recognize that they need to be employed as purely indicative of the deeper learning that has been the focus of the change.

Clearly the communication of the targets and their relationship to the focus of the change must be effectively managed to confirm the indicative nature of the targets. This means that the person leading the change, the subject leader, for example, will need to ensure that adequate training and discussion takes place so the all those participating in the initiative focus on and understand the core values rather than adopting a superficial stance around the meeting of the indicative targets.

ASK YOURSELF

- Am I able to distinguish between my indicative and actual targets?
- Do I have targets for which I have difficulty understanding the purpose?
- What opportunities do I have for explaining targets that I am setting for my subject on behalf of the school?

Effective monitoring

Once it is acknowledged that monitoring and evaluation are two distinct but related activities then progress can be made towards appreciating the forms and processes that, potentially, can be employed. Hardie (2001: 71) suggests four reasons for monitoring:

1 It allows you to assess how well you are doing.
2 It allows you to see where you are achieving targets and reaching standards.
3 It allows you to see where you are *not* achieving targets and reaching standards.
4 It shows you where you need to improve.

This is consistent with the ideal of a 'passion for improvement' inherent within the concept of total quality management (TQM) which places monitoring at the hub of a cycle of 'continuous improvement' (West-Burnham, 2002: 37). To be able to achieve such an outcome two prerequisites are required: systems and structures within the school to support the management of quality, and the staff with the experience and skills to be able to make value judgements. Subject-specific criteria for judging the quality of learning and teaching can be found in the preambles to the relevant NC subject documentation (DfES, 2004), which can be modified and adapted to suit the particular needs of the school.

By adopting a professional stance where the status quo is an unacceptable position, schools should gravitate towards a state of *kaizen* – a Japanese management concept which embodies a state of continuous improvement which every member of the school is actively engaged in. In effect this means that everybody monitors everything and offers suggestions as to how improvements can be brought about. *Kaizen* does not look for major initiative but simple ways of making minor improvements and alteration to the way things are done to smooth processes and clarify understanding. The key is in the communication and adoption of the suggestions to lead to a state of continuous transition towards the greater goals. In an attempt to develop a clear definition of the purposes and parameters of monitoring, Hardie (2001: 71) describes it as 'The planned routine gathering of useful information in a regular continuous and systematic checking process against previously set targets in order to take any necessary action'.

Within this definition are several key phrases and terms that warrant further amplification and examination. To start with it should be *planned*, built in through the bureaucratic processes and the responsibilities of the subject leaders and other promoted staff. It should not be perceived as being an additional burden but *routine*, effectively embedded into the culture of the school with active involvement on the part of all staff an accepted expectation. The whole process needs to be evidence driven making the *gathering of useful information* a focus of the activity. The question of what form this information might take will be addressed later in this chapter, but it should be stressed that it needs to be comparative in nature. The frequency of the monitoring is dependent upon a number of factors which will vary from situation to situation, but there does need to be a degree of *regularity* and, whether it is daily (attendance, for example), weekly (planning), half-termly (exercise books/marking), termly (lesson observation) or annually (pupil reports), a timescale needs to be indicated. Monitoring should be accepted as a *continuous* process focused upon the progression towards *previously set targets* where existing targets are being met and new ones formed on a rolling basis. To ensure that progress towards the targets is as direct as possible, monitoring will allow *necessary action* to be taken, in the form of adjustments to the targets or the course of action in order to keep on track.

Monitoring may range from the very formal to the informal depending upon the purpose of the process and who is performing it. Informal monitoring can be related to individual staff development where performance is being encouraged through a process of coaching. In this case it will usually be personal and internal to the school, with the subject leader assisting with the bespoke needs of a teacher, guiding him or her to an improved level of teaching competence. It will focus on process, examining the intrinsic value of the relationship to arrive at a deeper level of learning by being responsive to need. As it is emphasizing the development of the individual there will be a holistic, case-study approach with an audience based upon the internal needs of the school.

The formal approach to monitoring takes a much more impersonal perspective, focusing on the gathering of evidence which will be valid and credible beyond the classroom or school with an external audience. It will attempt to adopt a comparative approach to ensure that it is possible to generalize from the outcomes – essentially it will be judgemental, based upon explicit criteria in order to be objective and analytical in its response.

Kaizen suggests that monitoring should be a task that everybody involved in the school should be in a position to perform. While all stakeholders may be able to offer their perspective, it is unlikely that they will all be focusing directly on the goals the school has set. It may be that, as parents for example, they do not have full access to the information stream, or they are biased in favour of the immediate needs of their child – this possibly could be resolved through more effective communication. Governors have a key role to play in the monitoring process, but they may not have the time or the necessary training or understanding to appreciate fully the classroom activities that they are able to observe; indeed, Martin (2000) indicates that their involvement in the monitoring process need only be to ensure that it takes place! In order to track progress towards specific targets it is important for the monitoring to be consistent and based on a sound understanding of the targets; this would suggest that it would be most appropriate that key members of staff, who have these prerequisites, perform this role. Subject leaders are in the best position to judge the progression towards the targets that they have been involved in constructing.

But what should subject leaders and others be monitoring? In a word – everything. Clearly this is not particularly helpful, but at least defines the parameters with a reminder that almost anything that happens might be significant and worthy of note and attention. There should be an effort to construct levels of monitoring to ensure that time is used as effectively as possible. For an initiative that calls for teachers to adopt a more constructivist approach to teaching science through the use of open-ended questions, the first level of monitoring could simply be a check on attendance at the training session that introduced it; the next level may be to review lesson plans to see if teachers are identifying key open questions that they intend to ask their pupils; next could be a check on the written records that the pupils have produced of their science activities; followed by observation of teachers introducing tasks and teaching small groups; with a final check using assessment activities to determine whether the pupils have gained a better understanding of the science as a result of the intervention. At every stage of the monitoring process, if the subject leader is concerned about the feedback received, he or she can focus his or her attention and support on particular individuals. It is important that the monitoring process be agreed in advance so that teachers are expecting the checks and approach them constructively. For example, non-attendance at the training could be followed up through a quick chat in the staffroom to ensure that the teacher is aware of the expectations and that he or she feels adequately prepared for the initiative. A question mark over the quality of the pupils' written work or the teacher's comments on it might be resolved through the teaching of a model lesson and jointly assessing and commenting upon the resulting written work from pupils. The more the subject leader needs to intervene at an individual level the greater the impact will be for time allowances, so the onus is on the leader to ensure that the initial input and ongoing group support are sufficiently effective so that the monitoring process reveals that progress is as expected.

Monitoring has the potential to be a very threatening procedure, particularly for staff in a 'learning phase' and who are perhaps lacking in confidence in their own abilities. There are three considerations that a subject leader should take into account through the monitoring process:

1 *Reporting*: who is the audience for the evidence revealed through monitoring? To what extent is it confidential to the learner?
2 *Underachievement*: what are the consequences of individuals not being able to progress towards the acceptable standards that have been agreed?
3 *Overload*: are the expectations appropriate given other professional claims on teachers' time?

Ultimately, while monitoring should be regarded as a supportive activity to assist the learning of staff as part of a coaching scheme, it also has ramifications for professional enhancement. Teachers are expected to set themselves relevant and challenging professional targets and there needs to exist some process by which their progression towards them can be monitored and judged. In an attempt to avoid overloading the monitors, and to reduce the number of times that teachers are observed (mainly on grounds of cost), there may be pressures brought to bear to use classroom observations and other forms of monitoring for a dual purpose. This can seriously impair the relationship if not addressed constructively – teachers should be encourage to set challenging targets and attempt to try strategies beyond the norm, with the expectation that they will receive constructive feedback as a result, not worry about having to 'play safe' to get a positive observation.

- ◆ Are you aware of what is happening in your subject across the school?
- ◆ What evidence do you collect and how often do you collect it?
- ◆ What do you do in response to your analysis of evidence?
- ◆ How secure do you feel when being monitored?
- ◆ Do you feel that your school uses monitoring constructively and effectively?

Valuing what we do

Evaluation looks back in order to look forward. It attempts to analyse reality in respect of previously stated expectations and suggest revised actions (or expectations) as a result. Evaluation is a time-consuming exercise and for it to be a worthwhile activity, making effective use of time and resources, it will need to be acted upon – there is nothing to be gained by evaluating for the sake of producing an unread report, destined to gather dust on a shelf. For this reason, like monitoring, it needs to be a dynamic process as an integral element of a cycle of improvement. Preedy (2001: 89) defines curriculum evaluation as 'Concerned with gathering of evidence to describe and make judgement about the value or worth of curriculum plans, processes and outcomes, as a basis for developing and improving them'. However, in reality evaluation is not just for improvement (formative), it is also for compliance (summative). In addition to the questions evaluation asks about the achievement of goals and targets that the school has set for itself (what it 'wants' to do), it is also used for accountability to demonstrate that the school complies with minimum standards (what it 'must' do). For an evaluation to be effective it needs to operate on three levels, representing the three main dimensions of the curriculum: the intended (planned) curriculum, the offered (taught) curriculum and the received (learnt) curriculum – clearly an important aspect of any evaluation is the consistency between the three. External (summative) evaluation, a direct result of the centralization of curriculum control, is frequently presented in a condensed form – such as the use of 'league tables' for examination and assessment results, from which parents and the general public are expected to deduce the quality and effectiveness of the education offered by each school. An effective school would expect to meet if not exceed the external expectations placed upon it and so be able to concentrate its effort on the attainment of internally set stretch targets.

The overemphasis on immediate results from interventions, usually measured in terms of pupil achievement, can divert effort from more long-term and sustainable measures to improve performance. However, performance management techniques, which employ measures of pupil achievement (usually through standardized testing) as a target rather than an indicator, tend to encourage teachers to focus on short-term gains for pupils during that academic year rather than establishing a foundation for strong future development. With external accountability and, to an extent, teacher and headteacher salaries determined by narrow measures of 'success', the evaluation process has been forced to assume two, very different roles, one summative, for external consumption, and one developmental, for internal use. While the rational objective-based approach to evaluation, favoured by external evaluation frameworks, provides comparability through the use of simplistic standardized indicators it is not, directly, developmental. Research (Stoll and Fink, 1996; Hay McBer, 2000; Ofsted, 2004) suggests that schools can become more effective if they adopt particular characteristics in their operation and their leadership.

Ever since the work of Ralph Tyler in the 1930s and 1940s which adopted the use of product quality assurance methods from industry for schools in the USA, there has been the concentration on pupil performance as a means of measuring the quality of educational provision. The use of objective measures provided quantitative measures which can be used across all levels within education – from national targets to those for individual pupils. Process evaluation models adopts a more phenomenological stance, offering qualitative evidence based upon a wider range of evidence sources. While these data have the potential to be more informative and to provide opportunities for greater personal involvement and input from individual members of the school community, due to the qualitative nature of the evidence and the means of collection they must be regarded as less reliable. Because of these reliability issues, this approach to evaluation lacks the credibility of the quantitative approaches preferred by external agencies.

A further important difference between externally imposed evaluation and internal evaluation for development purposes is the ownership of the values. External evaluation imposes a set of objective values, which are generic for comparability purposes. For internal evaluation, the school's own value system, as presented in the mission statement and culture, will be used as the basis for judgements. However, it is likely that different stakeholders within the school will subscribe to different value systems and will have different priorities. To minimize these differences the leadership within the school (including the subject leaders) needs to communicate a vision with accompanying values that all stakeholders can appreciate, accept and take ownership of. In this situation the focus of evaluation is to ensure that the stated mission or vision for the school is appropriately reflected in what actually happens in the classroom – a comment from Ofsted is that it frequently does not!

What a school should aim to do is to develop a culture of inquiry which encompasses the whole school community. Schools should have a passion for learning, not just for pupils, but for all stakeholders, including the teaching staff. In the classroom teachers find it important for pupils to acknowledge weaknesses so that positive action can be taken. Senior management within schools need to perceive the teaching staff in a very similar way – with evaluation being a key tool for identifying strengths and weaknesses. Evaluation must be seen as a development tool aimed at bringing about improvement rather than a 'top-down' judgemental activity which is 'done to teachers' as part of a competence test. Developmental evaluation acknowledges the innate professionalism of the teaching staff where deficiencies are met with support and training opportunities, not sanctions. Teachers, through their professionalism, become accountable to each other, the contributions from each being valued by the whole in terms of how it contributes to the overall development and progress of the school.

As pupils are the focus of the work of a school, it is important to acknowledge their perspective within the evaluation process. Some of the evidence that they provide is derived from indirect means. Potentially, their success at school can be gauged by their academic achievements relative to expectations; the implication being that the more successful they are, the more satisfied they must be. Clearly there is much else for pupils to gain from attendance at school than narrow lines of academic development. Enjoyment, enthusiasm and social interaction may far outweigh the progress they are making on purely academic grounds, but the overall contribution that this is making to self-esteem and readiness for learning would be seriously undervalued using more conventional means of evaluation. The practice, in most primary schools, of pupils spending the majority of their time with one teacher, perhaps only changing teachers at the start of each school year, tightly links the pupils' perspective of the school to their perspective of the teacher. While the views of pupils, as end-users, are enormously important in terms of ensuring that learning and indeed the whole school experience is perceived as being as effective as possible, pupils can only base their judgement on what was received – they probably have no knowledge of what was planned.

Pupils and their parents are most concerned, according to MacBeath (1999), with the ethos (or school climate) and support for learning. MacBeath's research revealed five indicators which, combined, defined the quality of the school climate:

1 The school is a safe and happy place.
2 There are places for pupils to go and constructive things to do outside class time.

3 Pupils and staff behave in a relaxed and orderly way.
4 Pupils, staff and parents feel that their contributions to the school are valued.
5 The school is welcoming to visitors and newcomers (McBeath *et al.*, 1997: 37).

In order to avoid compromising the values of the school to meet the generic needs of external accountability, there must be a focus on evaluating what is important rather than what is easy to measure or externally required. A crucial factor in the long-term success of a school is its adherence to set of core values based upon its own agenda and its refusal to be diverted or overwhelmed by external pressures. The ownership of the issues and the belief in vision will encourage staff and the wider school community to invest effort in seeking success. Evaluation then becomes embedded in the development cycle as each year the school attempts to improve on the performance of the past year, focusing on their key priorities.

ASK YOURSELF

♦ Whose priorities am I evaluating against?
♦ Who is the audience for my subject evaluations?
♦ What action is expected as a result of my evaluation?

Summary: monitoring for support

Observing classroom performance provides the ideal opportunity to check that the planned curriculum is being effectively delivered and effectively received. To realize the potential of the opportunity time needs to be allotted either side of the observation to ensure that the purpose of, and focus for, the observation is clarified and there is an adequate opportunity to discuss the outcomes and devise developmental action plans. An observation is most effective when it is approached as a learning opportunity by both the observer and the observed. Both need to clarify their personal and professional objectives for the session and relate them to the developmental targets that have been set for the subject. The observer should state the purpose of the observation in terms of the key targets that have been set for the school as a whole, but if it is one of a series of observations that have been performed over an extended period of time then the purpose should relate to the content of the previous action plan. Adapting to this framework, the teacher who is being observed will ideally treat this as an opportunity to receive some constructive feedback and coaching in an area that he or she would benefit from developing his or her skills further. Within the overall development framework already identified for the subject and focused down by the subject leader, the teacher will identify two or three key objectives for him or herself for that session: skills or teaching strategies that he or she will attempt to employ.

References

DfES (Department for Education and Skills) (2004) *The National Curriculum for England*. London: HMSO (online at http://www.nc.uk.net/index.html).

DfES (2002) *Subject Leaders Key Reference Handbook*, London: DfES.

Hardie, B. (2001) 'Managing monitoring of the curriculum', in D. Middlewood and N. Burton (eds) *Managing the Curriculum*. London: Sage.

Hay McBer (2000) *Models of Excellence for School Leaders*. Nottingham: NCSL (online at http://stage.ncsl.org.uk/ncsl/index.cfm?pageid=hay-home2).

MacBeath, J. (1999) *Schools Must Speak for Themselves*. London: Routledge.

MacBeath, J., Boyde, B., Rand, J. and Bell, S. (1997) *Schools Must Speak for Themselves: Towards a Framework for Self-evaluation*. London: NUT.

Martin, J. (2000) 'Governors only have to ensure that monitoring takes place not do it themselves', *The Times Educational Supplement*, 16 June (online at www.tes.co.uk).

Ofsted (2004) *Information for Schools* (online at http://www.ofsted.gov.uk/schools/).

Preedy, M. (2001) 'Curriculum evaluation: measuring what we value', in D. Middlewood and N. Burton (eds) *Managing the Curriculum*. London: Sage.

Riley, K. and MacBeath, J. (2003) 'Effective Leaders and Effective Schools' in Bennett, N., Crawford, M. and Riches, C. (eds.) *Managing Change in Education*. Buckingham: Open University: 101–118.

Stake, R. (1976) *Evaluating Educational Programmes*. Paris: OECD.

Stoll, L. and Fink, D. (1996) *Changing our Schools*. Buckingham: Open University Press.

West-Burnham, J. (2002) *Managing Quality in Schools*. Harlow: Longman.

Recommended reading

Dean, J. (2003) *Subject Leadership in the Primary School*, London: David Fulton.

Website

Beacon Schools (2005) (http://www.standards.dfes.gov.uk/beaconschools/ search 'pupil progress monitoring evaluation'.

7

Accountability and the middle leader

LEARNING OUTCOMES OF THIS CHAPTER

By the end of this chapter you should be able to:

- understand the nature of schools as permeable organizations
- describe and analyse partnerships for learning, especially working with parents
- recognize and articulate the key features of accountability, especially in relation to school self-evaluation within the framework of the Ofsted inspection system

Schools as permeable organizations

The most important task for subject leaders is to ensure that the quality of teaching and learning is constantly monitored with clear signs of progress and an upward trend of achievement for *all* pupils (Brundrett and Terrell, 2004). This monitoring will key into the school improvement cycles outlined in the last chapter but it serves a further function which is to inform other stakeholders about the progress of the subject and, ultimately, of the school. Moreover, much of the literature on organizational theory reflects an increasing concern for the 'environment' that surrounds institutions. The open systems view goes so far as to suggest that organizations will always have some form of boundaries but that these are subject to being spanned, crossed or otherwise traversed in some manner. These ideas are especially important in the context of schools since schools have so many groups of people whom they wish to serve and to please. For this reason one interesting notion that is especially relevant to schools is the concept of *permeability*, by which we mean the ability for both egress and ingress of information, ideas, people and products. Since schools are set within a stakeholder community that includes not only staff and pupils but also parents, local and national authorities and society as a whole, schools are some of the most permeable organizations of all (Goldring, 1997: 290). It is, however, something of a bitter irony that this increasing need to develop links with the community comes at a time when schools are increasingly concerned about security in way that often leads to the construction of physical barriers to access. In this context it is ever more important that the aims and goals and day-to-day activities of the organization are communicated effectively both within and beyond the actual 'edges' of the school as a physical entity.

The role of subject leader within these overlapping communication structures and groupings is to occupy a middle management position within the school's hierarchical structure which provides a 'layer' of management between the senior management team (SMT) and those at the chalk face (Fleming and Amesbury, 2001: 2). Typically, in a traditional management model in secondary schools, subject leaders are positioned between classroom teachers and the head and SMT. No such layer exists in most primary schools, although larger primaries and middle schools may employ such staffing structures and even smaller primaries may have co-ordinators (or otherwise designated staff) who take a leading role in managing infant and junior departments. Such staff play a key role in helping to move a school forward in terms of its improvement plans, strategic development, overall goals and mission statement. They are also expected to ensure the smooth day-to-day running of the school's business and to monitor the progress of pupils and those staff within their department or subject team. Internally, subject leaders are accountable upwards to the head and SMT and downwards to the teachers in their subject team and the pupils they teach. They are also externally accountable to school governors, parents and less directly to education policy-makers and politicians. These accountability groupings are sometimes referred to as *stakeholders*, a term which is often used loosely to categorize 'all those who have a legitimate interest in the continuing effectiveness and success of an institution' (Waring, 1999: 180). However, the term could be equally well applied to pupils, departmental staff and key personnel higher up the chain of command, all of whom are internal to the institution and each of which have a legitimate interest in the effectiveness and success of an institution. A more helpful grouping recognizes that there are different interests and value systems depending on whether you are a pupil, a parent or a politician. For example, Becher *et al.* (1979) recognize that a teacher has three kinds of accountability: moral (to pupils and parents as clients); professionally (to one's colleagues); and contractual (to the school governing body and political masters). An emerging further type is market accountability, which is where clients have a choice of the institution they might attend. These sets of relationships serve a variety of functions but two are of especial relevance to this chapter:

1 *Partnerships for learning*: we argue that schools should be learning organizations and this can only become the case if parents and other carers are involved in the educational enterprise.
2 *Accountability*: schools must, by law, be accountable for their actions and performance as measured by the Ofsted inspection regime and performance indicators such as examination and assessment results.

Partnerships for learning: working with parents

Attitudes to parents have changed dramatically over the period of the last generation of teachers. It was once not uncommon that the prevailing view of teachers and headteachers was that parents were firmly encouraged to stay outside the school gates – leaving the process of education to teachers who acted as autonomous professionals in their own classrooms. It might be too dramatic to say that the gates have been thrown open in recent years (although that is true in some schools) but it is certainly true that there has been a gradual and developing belief that parents should be encouraged to be intimately involved in their child's education, both at home and in school. This new attitude has, in part, been thrust upon schools because the new, more market-driven ideology of education, exemplified in the Education Acts 1988 and 1992, gave parents the opportunity to choose which school they sent their child to. To some extent such choice is actually illusory since there are often insufficient places in the most popular schools to take the number of children whose parents would like to send them to attend the school. Nonetheless, the overall impact of the removal of fixed catchment areas has been one whereby schools leaders have had to think very carefully about whether or not they are pleasing both pupils and parents in a way which would not have been the case in earlier periods.

The imperative to involve parents has increased as both governmental initiatives and educational research have increasingly stressed the role of parents in enhancing learning. Since 1994 Ofsted have investigated the level of involvement of parents in a school's life and their attitude to their children's schools and the white paper, *Excellence in Schools* (DfEE, 1997), stressed the importance of parents as co-educators with teachers and the pupils themselves. These notions about parental involvement in learning had initial impact especially in the area of literacy since a number of studies have shown the importance of the family in creating a home environment that would support children's learning in school and beyond (see, for instance, Hannon, 2000). Such ideas began to impact on national policy in the late 1990s when the Literacy Task Force stated that 'Parents have a vital role in supporting and encouraging children's learning, perhaps most of all in helping that child to read' (1997: 32). The subsequent National Literacy Strategy and Numeracy Strategy incorporated parental engagement as a central element of their approach, and the overall National Primary Strategy, embodied in *Excellence and Enjoyment* (DfES, 2003: 47), states that 'partnership with parents is critical to helping children to achieve as well as they possibly can'.

The National Strategy also symbolizes a move beyond links with parents to a broader agenda of 'joined-up thinking' which seeks to integrate the whole community into the education of children. The strategy suggests that detailed parental involvement strategies be developed locally, so that they really meet local needs, and goes on to state that support should be co-ordinated through local preventative strategies, which bring together all those agencies responsible for services for children, young people and families (DfEE, 2003: 48–9). Taking this as the starting point the National Strategy (2003: 49–50) suggests that parental engagement should:

- Build on Sure Start and other early years programmes, particularly as children transfer from early years settings to school, so that it is clear to parents that they still have an important role.
- Support parents in helping their children learn – through family learning projects and also support for parenting skills.
- Take a multi-agency approach to supporting parents in engaging with their children's learning.
- Make it clear that parents have responsibilities too.

This commitment to communities of learning is underpinned by the notion of 'extended schools' which support standards because they take a wider approach to supporting children's learning, with more opportunities for out-of-hours learning, that help build schools into the fabric of the local community by offering easy access to a range of educational and other services for children, families and other members of the community. The government's aim is that, over time, all schools will provide at least some of these services, and some schools will go further and offer a comprehensive range of activities and support. It is envisaged that each full service school will offer a prescribed core of childcare, study support, family and lifelong learning, health and social care, parenting support, sports and arts facilities, and ICT access (DfEE, 2003: 51).

The notion of working with parents is, however, more complex than the exhortations for involvement might suggest. At the most pragmatic and practical level parents may well be disinclined to be involved in their children's schools, perhaps because of their own experiences in education (Merchant and Marsh, 1998; Osler *et al.*, 2000). The concept of extended schools is laudable but it presents ever more challenges to the leadership of schools, at all levels, at a time when multiple innovations are already problematic and time-consuming. Schools need to ensure that they ask key questions in order to facilitate this movement towards wider engagement. Edwards and Waring (1999) suggest a number of implications for practitioners when seeking to involve parents:

- Does your home–school policy have a clear rationale for parental involvement?
- Is your rationale for parental involvement all about school-led demands?
- Do you have a way of finding out what parents think about their child, their child's education and what they view as important?
- What does the school ask parents to do with children? Does this build on what parents know and can do?
- Does the school know if its strategies for parental involvement contribute to increased learning?
- Are the tasks parents are asked to do equally accessible for all parents?
- Do the teachers have an opportunity to find out what parents can contribute and how they see their children's schooling?
- Are parent workshops planned with the needs of the parents in mind?

Overall the enhanced interest in parental and wider community engagement in education is to be applauded since it links with developing research findings about the nature of learning. The increasing engagement of governmental bodies in such an initiative is also to be welcomed since it provides impetus and focus for such initiatives but subject leaders, who will play a key role in developing such relationships, must be aware of the inherent challenges that they face in integrating parents and the wider community into networks of support.

Case study

Gawsworth Primary School is situated in a rural village location three miles south of Macclesfield in east Cheshire. The school has some 190 pupils in seven single-age classes and it employs nine teachers, including the head. The local area is comparatively wealthy and there are several private schools nearby but pupils come from a wide range of types of households. Gawsworth enjoys a good reputation for standards and its broad, balanced curriculum, and a very high percentage of the pupils come from outside the catchment.

The school has always fostered links with parents but in recent years has expanded their involvement considerably. A vibrant, active and high-profile PTA is the core of parental activity and it organizes events within and outside school, which vary from fundraising dances to communal bingo evenings and cinema screenings for the children. Such is the power of the PTA's efforts that because of them the school enjoys considerable resources. Their latest plan is to buy interactive whiteboards for all classes. Various subcommittees of the PTA operate at a smaller scale on specific projects as well as raising the school profile in the local media. The governing body has a high parental representation and this has led to meaningful hands-on roles for some in school planning and development.

The school communicates with parents in a variety of ways, through the PTA, letters, website, surveys and regular meetings, detailing curriculum, policy and achievements. Parental support is strong throughout the school and each class has a parent who acts as liaison when volunteers are needed in numbers – such as for the annual fete or Christmas. The school positively encourages parents to become deeply involved in their child's education from first contact when the pupils attend on preschool visits. Traditional parental helpers are active in every class, performing a variety of tasks from hearing readers to group work in practical activities. Key parents are encouraged to be responsible for ongoing projects, under teacher supervision, such as maintaining the library or reading scheme. Yet more have registered particular skills or hobbies that they are willing to share with the children. Beyond the classroom their support on visits is vital. As adult/child ratios are constantly revised, parents take an active part in sporting activities, running training and coaching sessions as well as establishing an annual Cycling Proficiency Scheme.

Teachers can expect regular and varied contact with parents from a casual cup of coffee in the staffroom to more formal arrangements via twice-yearly parents' evenings. Parents are informed each year of curriculum topics by their child's teacher. Homework and reading diaries have space for parental comments/teacher communication and this facility is used frequently. Reports are issued for parents once a year, and there is also more targeted learning for those children with special needs, whose parents have regular review meetings with staff. The school also seeks parental opinions on its progress through an annual survey, the information from which is collated and significant development points are acted on. Parental opinion and action can be considerable as the school found when the education authority tried to cancel the free pupil bus service. Such was the outcry the threat was immediately withdrawn.

A recent development is the establishment of courses within school for parents who may wish to develop ICT skills. This is run in conjunction with a local college of further education. If successful more variation may follow.

All this gives a feeling of partnership rather than just the traditional teacher/parent relationship. Where once the presence of parents in the classroom may have been the cause of a curiously raised eyebrow, now it would be impossible to function without them.

No one entering teaching should be in any doubt parents are going to be as much a part of their job as the children. (*Source*: Simon Jones, senior teacher, Gawsworth Primary School, Cheshire.)

External accountability and Ofsted inspection

The Education Reform Act 1988 replaced the principles of universalism and social equality enshrined in the 1944 Act with the ideology of the market via individualism, public choice and accountability. Indeed it can be argued that accountability is the concomitant of enabling schools to become market driven and self-managing. Decentralization has been viewed as a key method to improve efficiency, not only in schools but across all organizations. Yet central government must continue to monitor what goes on in schools in order to ensure that they are improving and, in turn, to be accountable to their electorate. Accountability can thus be regarded as a counterpart of the greater freedom at institutional level (Anderson, 2005: 75). It is important to remember that accountability can take different forms, and Halstead (1994) suggests six different models:

1 The central control model (contractual, employer dominant).
2 The self-accounting model (contractual, professional dominant).
3 The consumerist model (contractual, consumer dominant).

4 The chain of responsibility model (responsive, employer dominant).
5 The professional model (responsive, professional dominant).
6 The partnership model (responsive, consumer dominant).

These varying forms of accountability may be seen as a continuum from local, professionally dominated systems to the kind of externally driven systems which appear to have dominated the early Ofsted model. Scott (1999) draws on the work of Halstead and considers five models of accountability, one of which, the *evaluative state model*, was particularly applicable to state primary and secondary schools until a re-evaluation of the Ofsted framework in the late 1990s. Within this model, the state gives over the precise implementation of policy to semi-independent bodies such as Ofsted which, while accountable to government ministers, over-ride existing forms of accountability such as LEA–school relations (Duncan, 2004). In this model, the inspection process itself becomes the means by which schools comply with government policy (Scott, 1999: 27). With its regular cycle of inspections and severe sanctions for failing and underperforming schools, Ofsted has been granted significant powers to compel schools to conform to government prescriptions on its behalf. Despite the externality and apparent rigour and clarity of this system, Scott (1999: 30) claimed that 'systems of accountability ... can never be imposed absolutely. There is, in other words, space within any imposed model for local initiative'. Thus school managers were undoubtedly proactive in seeking to influence the accountability structures by finding ways of managing and controlling the inspection process in ways which better served the interests of school staff, parents and pupils. Such schools have learned to use external accountability systems to their advantage as well as to improve and develop themselves.

Nonetheless, the Ofsted model of external scrutiny of schools has been subject to a sustained critique since its inception in the early 1990s. The regime has been criticized both for its practical efficacy in raising standards of achievement and, more conceptually, for its flawed and sometimes inimical attitudes to efficiency and effectiveness. Early follow-up studies revealed that few school development plans rooted in inspection findings actually followed through on the issues identified in the inspection process despite the fact that most staff accepted the issues identified needed to be addressed (Gray and Wilcox, 1995; Silcock and Brundrett, 2002: 64). Moreover, it has been suggested that the Ofsted school inspection regime, especially as it existed in its first iteration, conflated the two concepts of efficiency and effectiveness without unpacking the complex inter-relationships usually existing between them (Fielding, 1997: 11) in that schools can be effective but profoundly inefficient if they 'add value' to student experience at unacceptable cost. Equally, schools can be efficient but ineffective if they arrange schooling at minimal cost but fail to educate students. Moreover one must question the nature of a school's efficiency if it leads to burgeoning workloads and surveillance for and of teachers (Ball, 1990). As Fielding (1997: 12) points out, any recognition of the 'non-neutral' status of efficiency begs the question as to whose interests shape the nature and process of work. Market-led visions of schooling exclude any exploration of the potentially problematic nature of the curriculum. School work is usually seen as dealing with a fixed, immutable body of knowledge, with any alterations justified according to the dominant paradigm of increased effectiveness (Silcock and Brundrett, 2002: 225). It is, however, important to remember no particular model of accountability is static or immutable since systems of accountability are value-laden and can change, depending on the particular historical and political circumstances of the time (Duncan, 2004). The latter part of the 1990s saw a subtle shift in the relationship between Ofsted and the schools that they inspected from a hard-edged external system to a more inclusive set of practices which increasingly took account of the views of the school's leadership team.

This new form of inspection is more contingent on school self-evaluation, a fact that adds further weight to arguments in favour of democratic or co-constructive teaching that are discussed in Chapter 11. The point to stress is that co-constructive teaching depends on ongoing critical self-evaluation: generalizing from ongoing particular circumstances to gain a picture of any one school's achievements should be a fairly straightforward business (Silcock and Brundrett, 2002: 177). The new approach is embodied in *Inspecting Schools: Framework for Inspecting Schools* (Ofsted, 2003b: 3) which outlines key principles, including the following:

- Inspection acts in the interests of children, young people and adult learners and, where relevant, their parents, to encourage high-quality provision that meets diverse needs and promotes equality.
- Inspection is evaluative and diagnostic, assessing quality and compliance, and providing a clear basis for improvement.
- The purpose of inspection and the procedures to be used are communicated clearly to those involved.
- Inspection invites and takes account of any self-evaluation by those inspected.
- Inspection informs those responsible for taking decisions about provision.
- Inspection is carried out by those who have sufficient and relevant professional expertise and training.
- Evidence is recorded and is of sufficient range and quality to secure and justify judgements.
- Judgements are based on systematic evaluation requirements and criteria, are reached corporately where more than one inspector is involved and reflect a common understanding in Ofsted about quality.

- Effectiveness is central to judging the quality of provision and processes.
- Inspection includes clear and helpful oral feedback and leads to written reporting that evaluates performance and quality, and identifies strengths and areas for improvement.
- The work of all inspectors reflects Ofsted's stated values and its code of conduct.
- Quality assurance is built into all inspection activities to ensure that these principles are met and inspection is improved.

In law, inspections must report on the following:

1 The educational standards achieved in the school.
2 The quality of the education provided by the school.
3 The quality of leadership and management, including whether the financial resources made available to the school are managed efficiently.
4 The spiritual, moral, social and cultural development of pupils at the school.

The *Evaluation Schedule* in Part C of the *Framework* covers these four requirements by requiring inspectors to evaluate the following aspects of the school's work:

- Standards achieved.
- Pupils' attitudes, values and personal development.
- Teaching and learning.
- The quality of the curriculum.
- The care, guidance and support of pupils.
- Partnerships with parents, other schools and the community.
- Leadership and management.
- The areas of learning, subjects and courses of the curriculum.
- Other matters that HMCI may specify.

It is intended that inspection helps the school by providing an overall judgement on the effectiveness of the school, and by identifying its strengths and weaknesses and the most important points for improvement. Within this new formulation there is a welcome recognition of the notion of schools monitoring their own performance.

What part does school self-evaluation play in inspection?

Schools have a range of internal processes for monitoring their own performance and evaluating the effectiveness of their work in raising achievement. Such monitoring and evaluation should contribute, directly or indirectly, to periodic updating of the school improvement plan, which maps the priorities for action and sets out programmes for implementing them. Inspection takes account of or contributes to these processes in several ways:

- A brief self-evaluation report (*Form S4*) prepared by the school helps to focus inspection effort where it matters most and to respond to any specific issues that the inspection can usefully include. The school's summary of its self-evaluation is used as the basis for discussion between the lead inspector and the headteacher and, where possible, governors of the school, when the inspection is being planned.
- The quality and use made of school self-evaluation are a good indication of the calibre of management. Evidence of how effectively schools undertake self-evaluation and the use they make of it helps inspectors to evaluate the quality of management in the school and the capacity of the school to improve.

In order to promote the use of self-evaluation, the self-evaluation report (*Form S4*), which is completed by the school before inspection, is constructed so as to match the *Evaluation Schedule* used by inspectors. Many schools use the *Evaluation Schedule* as the basis for their internal evaluation processes (see Figure 7.1). The lead inspector must allow sufficient time, both in the school before the inspection and in preparation, to analyse and interpret the

---

Effectiveness of the school

1   How successful is the school?
2   What should the school do to improve?

Standards achieved by pupils

3.1 How high are standards achieved in the areas of learning, subjects and courses of the curriculum?
3.2 How well are pupils' attitudes, values and other personal qualities developed?

Quality of education provided by the school

4   How effective are teaching and learning?
5   How well does the curriculum meet pupils' needs?
6   How well are pupils cared for, guided and supported?
7   How well does the school work in partnership with parents, other schools and the community?

Leadership and management of the school

8   How well is the school led and managed?
9   How good is the quality of education in areas of learning, subjects and courses?
10 What is the quality of other specified features?

Figure 7.1 *Evaluation schedule*: contents
Source: Ofsted (2003b: 29)

school's performance, to identify issues and themes, and to design and plan the inspection so that it will reflect the essence of the school. This process must be thorough and consultative (Ofsted, 2003b: 10).

Ofsted has also published the following ten-point checklist that schools can use to evaluate their own commitment to education for sustainable development (ESD) (Ofsted, 2003a: Annex C):

1 Could the school promote a culture and ethos which values the development, knowledge, attitudes and skills in pupils to enable them to participate individually and collectively to improve the quality of life in a sustainable way?

2 Has the school produced a policy statement for ESD which sets out the aims, priorities and targets for promoting ESD as a whole-school initiative, and identified strategies to promote and raise the profile of ESD within the school and the wider school community? Has it co-ordinated and monitored ESD initiatives and activities throughout the school to ensure a consistency of approach?

3 Is there a programme of staff development in place to raise awareness of ESD and develop teachers' competency and skills?

4 Have subject leaders identified opportunities within their schemes of work to enable ESD to be delivered and reinforced through the curriculum? Does the teaching approach promote active learning to develop pupils' understanding of sustainable development?

5 Does the school develop active and responsible citizenship and stewardship through pupils' involvement in active decision-making through a school council or eco-committee?

6 What links has the school established to support and develop a global and international dimension within the curriculum?

7 How does the school involve, and make use of, the wider school community to enrich learning and pupils' personal and social development including the effective use of business, local authorities, non-government organisations and community groups to support their work in developing the sustainable agenda?

8 In what ways does the school respect and value diversity?

9 In what active ways is the school involved in improving performance against sustainability indicators, including waste management, fair trade and a green purchasing policy?

10 Has the school embarked on, or maintained, a programme of ground development and improvement to support learning, promote stewardship and improve the quality of life?

Whatever demands are made upon subject teams with respect to account-ability, the central focus must remain firmly on teaching and learning since this is the key to successful curriculum teams. However, there is now a new emphasis on the importance of all schools becoming *inclusive* schools. Since 2001, Ofsted school inspectors have received additional training to ensure that procedures for monitoring and inspecting entitlement for *all* pupils are tightened up. This not only means that there need to be robust systems in place to ensure that pupils with special educational needs have full access to the curriculum but that the progress and well-being of pupils are not impeded or negatively affected by incidents of bullying and racism. This matters as much for the particular subject as it does for the school as a whole. Indeed, there is an important reference in the National Standards for Subject Leadership (TTA, 1998: 5(B) (vii) (xi), p. 11) which mentions the need for high expectations and success with pupils with special educational needs and linguistic needs as well as the requirement to ensure that teachers of the subject know how to recognize and deal with racial stereotyping.

The essence of successful subject leader accountability

The environment that schools are operating within today is part of a new culture of accountability, which is affecting most of the public sector. It demands increasing amounts of information, comparative data and target-setting without necessarily helping professionals to account for their practices and achievement in ways which parents, pupils and school gover-nors might find interesting and helpful. One of the things which successful schools have done in recent years is to learn to control and manage account-ability in ways which serve the interests of teachers, pupils and parents as well as the school community as a whole. It therefore matters that teacher managers do not blindly acquiesce to its prescriptions as though they were mere technicians. Their professional knowledge, experience and wisdom need to inform every stage of the process because this is an important source of informed 'truth' which makes accountability of any kind make sense.

Following on from this, one of the key requirements of subject leaders is to adopt an attitude and mindset which ensure that they control the process without letting it control them. Whatever paper systems and planning for-mats are used, certain fundamental principles should remain sacrosanct and these essentially concern the pupils, staff, parents and the school as a whole.

The point of any accountability system must be to tell the truth, simply, clearly and in an open and transparent way (Brundrett and Terrell, 2004).

This means that pupils are taught well, know what they need to do in order to improve, are prepared well for examinations and are enthusiastic about the subject. It means that parents are well informed about their children's achievements, know what is being done to help them if they are having difficulties and how they can support what the school is doing. As far as the subject team or department is concerned, it means ensuring that everyone works together as a team, knows and understands the broad and smaller picture in terms of the subject's development and has a clear sense of direction.

Moreover, each individual's effort is recognized and valued and the team is kept up to date and fully informed of changes and new external initiatives. This collective endeavour needs then to be carefully aligned with the school's aims and mission statement so that policy is translated into practice through 'a logical progression from policy formulation to policy implementation within the planning hierarchy' (Giles, 1997).

ASK YOURSELF

◆ Who are the key groups of stakeholders that relate to your school and department?
  – Consider the different needs and requirements of these groups or individuals.
  – Consider to what extent these needs are complementary or clashing.
◆ Identify the methods, both formal and informal, by which these groups or individuals are informed and consulted about developments in your subject area and consider how these could be enhanced.

Summary

In conclusion, subject leaders need to keep at the front of their minds that their work in accountability has both a professional and moral dimension. An ability to handle bureaucracy and to keep up to date with paperwork is clearly important but of far greater significance is their ability to engage teachers, pupils and parents in the accounting process in ways which demonstrate trust and belief in their versions of the truth. The way may then be open for them to work towards their version of *intelligent* accountability (Brundrett and Terrell, 2004).

To be successful at accountability subject leaders need to be strong on paper systems and to be able to produce spreadsheets and data sources as a matter of course. If manageable, user-friendly ways of dealing with the paperwork can be found, it then becomes easier to focus on the more important aspects of the task. These include being proactive and ahead of the game so that new initiatives and demands can be anticipated without becoming yet another burden. New developments and improvements needed for the subject need to be made with an eye on the strategy, mission, aims and vision of the whole school. Most important of all is the team itself, which needs to feel a collective ownership of the vision and the direction in which the subject is moving. This means that individual members of the team need to be given specific areas of responsibility which draw upon their respective strengths and qualities. The concept of *distributive leadership* is an important concept in the more recent literature on schools facing challenging contexts (see, especially, Gray, 2000; Harris, 2002). Quite simply, this means that responsibility is devolved throughout the schools so that there are many rather than a few leaders. The power of praise, involving others in decision-making and giving professional autonomy to individual teachers are examples of some its most effective strategies. This approach to leadership can be equally well applied to the subject team.

References

Anderson, L. (2005) 'Decentralization, autonomy and school improvement', in M. Coleman and P. Earley (eds) *Leadership and Management in Education: Cultures, Change and Context*. Oxford: Oxford University Press.

Ball, S.J. (1990) 'Management as a moral technology', in S.J. Ball (ed.) *Foucault and Education*. London: Routledge.

Becher, T., Eraut, M., Barton, J., Canning, T. and Knight, J. (1979) *Accountability in the Middle Years of Schooling: An Analysis of Policy Options. Final Report of the East Sussex LEA/University of Sussex Research Project*. Brighton: University of Sussex.

Boyd, W. (1997) 'Environmental pressures and competing paradigms in educational management', *ESRC Seminar Series Paper*, Leicester, June.

Brundrett, M. and Terrell, I. (eds) (2004) *Learning to Lead in the Secondary School: Becoming and Effective Head of Department*. London: RoutledgeFalmer.

Bush, T. (1999) 'The vanishing boundaries: the importance of effective external relations', in J. Lumby and N. Foskett (eds) *Managing External Relations in Schools and Colleges*. London: Paul Chapman Publishing.

DfEE (1997) *Excellence in Schools*. London: HMSO.

DfES (2003) *Excellence and Enjoyment: A Strategy for Primary Schools*. London: DfES.

Duncan, D. (2004) 'Subject leader accountability', in M. Brundrett and I. Terrell (eds) *Learning to Lead in the Secondary School: Becoming an Effective Head of Department*. London: RoutledgeFalmer.

Edwards, A. and Waring, J. (1999) 'Parental involvement in raising the achievement of primary school pupils: why bother?', *Oxford Review of Education*, 25: 325–41.

Fielding, M. (1997) 'Beyond school effectiveness and school improvement: lighting the slow fuse of possibility', *Curriculum Journal*, 8: 7–27.

Fleming, P. and Amesbury, M. (2001) *The Art of Middle Management in Primary Schools*. London: David Fulton.

Giles, C. (1997) *School Development Planning: A Practical Guide to the Strategic Management Process*. London: Northcote House.

Goldring, E.B. (1997) 'Educational leadership: schools, environments and boundary spanning', in M. Preedy *et al.* (eds) *Educational Management: Strategy, Quality and Resources*. Buckingham: Open University Press.

Gray, J. (2000) *Causing Concern but Improving: A Review of Schools' Experience*. London: DfEE.

Gray, J. and Wilcox, B. (1995) *Good School, Bad School*. Buckingham: Open University Press.

Halstead, M. (1994) 'Accountability and values', in D. Scott (ed.) *Accountability and Control in Educational Settings*. London: Cassell.

Hannon, P. (2000) 'Rhetoric and research in family literacy', *British Educational Research Journal*, 26: 121–38.

Harris, A. (2002) 'Effective leadership in schools facing challenging contexts', *School Leadership and Management*, 22: 15–26.

Literacy Task Force (1997) *The Implementation of the National Literacy Strategy*. London: DfEE.

Maclure, S. (1994) 'Act of faith amid the heart of battle', *The Times Educational Supplement*, 6 May.

Merchant, G. and Marsh, J. (1998) *Co-ordinating Primary Language and Literacy: The Subject Leader's Handbook*. London: Paul Chapman Publishing.

Ofsted (2003a) *Taking the first step forward ... Towards an Education for Sustainable Development* (Annex C). London: Ofsted.

Ofsted (2003b) *Inspecting Schools: Framework for Inspecting Schools*. London: HMSO.

O'Neill, O. (2002) *A Question of Trust*. Reith Lecture Two, BBC Radio 4, 23 April.

Osler, A., Watling, R. and Busher, H. (2000) *Reasons for Exclusion from School: Report to the DfEE*. Leicester: Centre for Citizenship, School of Education, University of Leicester.

Scott, D. (1999) 'Accountability in education systems', in J. Lumby and N. Foskett (eds) *Managing External Relations in Schools and Colleges.* London: Paul Chapman Publishing.

Silcock, P. and Brundrett, M. (2002) *Competence, Success and Excellence in Teaching.* London: RoutledgeFalmer.

TTA (1998) *National Standards for Subject Leaders.* London: Teacher Training Agency.

Waring, S. (1999) 'Finding your way: sensing the external environment', in J. Lumby and N. Foskett (eds) *Managing External Relations in Schools and Colleges.* London: Paul Chapman Publishing.

Recommended reading

Glatter, R. (2002) 'Governance, autonomy and accountability in education', in T. Bush and L. Bell (eds) *The Principles of Educational Management.* London: Paul Chapman Publishing.

Lumby, J. and Foskett, N. (eds) *Managing External Relations in Schools and Colleges.* London: Paul Chapman Publishing (pp. 179–92).

Scott, D. (ed.) (1994) *Accountability and Control in Educational Settings.* London: Cassell.

Websites

Advisory Centre for Education (http://www.ace-ed.org.uk/).

Ofsted (2003) *Inspecting Schools: Framework for Inspecting Schools* (http://www.ofsted.gov.uk/publications/docs/3266.pdf).

The Parent Centre (http://www.parentcentre.gov.uk/).

The Primary National Strategy (http://www.standards.dfes.gov.uk/ primary/about/).

SECTION C

Working with Resources

8

Identifying and organizing learning resources

LEARNING OUTCOMES OF THIS CHAPTER

By the end of this chapter you should be able to:

- describe the nature of learning resources
- understand the importance of the resource audit and of maintaining resources
- articulate and analyse the role of the subject leader as resource manager, especially in the organization of learning resources
- recognize the importance of people as a resource

The nature of learning resources

Everything that can be utilized by the school to deliver the curriculum and enhance learning is a resource worthy of consideration. This chapter will focus on the effective use and deployment of resources from an organizational perspective; the succeeding chapter will explore the financial implications of resource decisions.

The subject leader will need to make him or herself aware of the resources that may have a direct or indirect bearing on the ability of teachers in the school to support learning in the subject area. There are various ways in which the resources can be categorized and organized from an identification perspective depending on their durability, degree of specialism and format – and in many respects all these need to be applied for the resources to be effectively managed.

While some resources are designed to be consumed during the course of teaching (such as pencils, workbooks, cooking ingredients) others are expected to be more durable and reused, but it still must be acknowledged that there will come a time when they too will need to be repaired and or replaced. Textbooks become 'dated', computers outmoded, PE equipment dangerous with wear and tear, science and design and technology equipment broken or worn out – so all resources, in the short to long term, will be subject to planned renewal.

Often the location of resources will be determined by their frequency of use or degree of specialism. Some resources are an essential element of many different subjects and so will need to be provided for each classroom – this is particularly true of resources used for measuring, recording or presenting. Some subject, such as mathematics and English, are taught throughout the week and may require some specialist resources to be constantly available in classrooms. Some schools will have specialist areas for some subjects, such as PE, resulting in the specialist PE resources being stored in that area. Other subjects may require specialist equipment to be brought to classrooms, so organization, storage and mobility become prime considerations. Musical instruments may be required in each classroom during the week, necessitating the careful timetabling of all classes for music to ensure availability. Other subjects, such as science, may require specialist equipment and materials to be available in a classroom for the duration of a module of work – again requiring careful planning and timetabling but on a longer timescale. Some equipment has an ambiguity in its degree of specialism and will need to be organized to reflect the way in which the school approaches learning in that area. ICT, for example, might be devolved to classrooms on an equal footing (each classroom having, at its immediate disposal, a number of computers), or it might be taught in a specialist suite which classes will be timetabled for (perhaps with 'spare' machines devolved to classrooms). Increasingly, the use of laptops, wirelessly networked to mobile units, is being used to bring the computer suite to the classroom.

The format of the resource will frequently dictate how it is to be organized, maintained and made available to the school. Paper-based resources are often the easiest for the subject leader to identify, organize and disseminate. Most school staff will be familiar with library-based information organization and retrieval systems with a cataloguing system based upon the subject content of the resource. Clearly CD, DVD and video can be categorized in much the same way. Physical equipment, depending on how robust or large it is, may need to be organized in more specialized ways.

There are two further formats: people and places. People, as a resource, will be addressed in greater detail below, acknowledging the crucial role that non-teachers can play in enhancing the effectiveness of the curriculum. The most obvious 'place' that can be regarded as a resource is the classroom itself. The subject leader should be in a position to advise on how the classroom can be arranged to support the learning taking place; this could be in terms of the positioning and use of the furniture and also the nature and form of displays (in general, classroom display space should be used to stimulate and enhance current learning, with more public areas being used to present completed work).

While not an issue for a subject leader, the general quality of an area of the school may be of particular importance to a key stage, phase or year group leader. The school's expenditure on cleaning, lighting, heating and décor may, initially, be taken as a lower educational priority than exercise books, but it has profound implications for the quality of learning and teaching. When classrooms are not at an appropriate temperature, or the quality of the lighting is poor (too dim or bright), it will reduce the ability of the children to learn – without a basic level of comfort the learning processes suffer. Classrooms need ventilation, shade from the sun, access to drinking water – and year heads need to ensure that the classrooms they have been allocated have the basic facilities. While classroom décor may not be an obvious priority, from an educational perspective, it is an important factor in instilling a sense of pride in the children (and their teachers!) – that they are valued and worthy of a bright and attractive learning environment. Clearly it also conveys an important message to those who visit the school (including existing and potential parents).

Individual teachers are firmly in control of the overall state of their classrooms and need to be encouraged to conform to the standards expected within the school. Murphy (1994) suggests that devolving too much autonomy to individual teachers can lead to issues of 'ownership' of particular classrooms, leading to problems when classes or teachers need to be redeployed to other teaching accommodation resulting in 'politically sensitive' situations. This could lead to a lack of internal movement and stagnation of ideas and approaches to learning as teachers lean into a comfort zone.

The fabric of the building and surrounding grounds offers the school a means of conveying a message to the local community and school visitors about the priorities and values of the school. Establishing a 'corporate image' through a coherent use of colour, décor and furnishings alongside an underpinning ethos can be a very expensive process, even through a rolling renewal. However, much can be achieved by adopting a particular colour scheme, or approach to display. Clearly, though, this is an issue to be addressed through a central budget.

The actual teaching environment, the classrooms and any shared areas should be arranged and organized to maximize the potential of the curriculum that is taught and teaching strategies that are employed. Where the aim is to foster an independent approach to learning, it is clearly desirable for the classroom layouts to be conducive to and supportive of this style of learning. Furniture will need to be set out to allow pupils to gain direct access to the equipment and materials that they require, within the bounds of health and safety and effective classroom management.

Kelly and Kedney (1992: 146) have identified five barriers that might be placed in the way of redeveloping the learning environment:

1 Lack of accountability.
2 Lack of information.
3 Too much information.
4 Inappropriate territoriality.
5 Short-term thinking.

Clarity of thought and action will minimize inertia although there could be dissenting voices, from other teachers, on the grounds of perceived favourable funding towards the classrooms or areas initiating the improvement, but not for the improvements themselves. If work on shared areas is prioritized it should signal an important message to other teachers looking enviously on! The effect of the rejuvenation process in the more public areas, while probably at the expense of the purchase of more directly recognizable learning resources, is to demonstrate that the whole school can begin to benefit and move forwards.

The school grounds should be assessed to consider how they might be used to support learning in the subject. The more that can be done to link pupils' learning from in the classroom to opportunities outside it, the more likely they will be able to apply their learning to other contexts. Finally, opportunities to visit local features should be identified (and risk assessed) as well as more distant educational centres which are designed to enhance learning in specific areas (again, risk assessed with details of any additional costs specified).

Once the subject leader is aware of the types of resource that might exist, an audit should be performed to identify and catalogue what is currently available in school.

ASK YOURSELF

- ◆ Is my school making the best use of the space that it has?
- ◆ Does my classroom help or hinder they way I want the children to learn?
- ◆ What does the classroom (and school) say about the way we work?

Resource audit

According to Burton (2004: 183), there are two ways to approach a resource audit, either 'starting from *the resources* you have got, or, alternatively, starting from a "zero-base" and identifying what you need' for the intended curriculum. Unless a subject leader is starting with a 'blank sheet' – either a new school or completely rethinking the curriculum – then the former, rather than the latter, approach is the one to adopt. However, this does mean that thinking may be constrained by what is available rather than what is desirable – i.e. what question is being used to focus the activity:

- What do we want to do?
- How can we use this?

Burton expressed it in these terms: 'Does the availability of resources determine the curriculum, or does the curriculum determine the organisation and acquisition of resources?' (2004: 183). While it would be foolish to restrict the curriculum to what can be currently resourced, it would be equally unwise to disregard expensive specialist equipment on the grounds that it does not fully meet the needs of the envisaged approach to learning and teaching – compromises will need to be found. Existing resources will have to be taken into account when new purchases are being made to ensure compatibility. This could very well mean that preferred resources will have to be forgone in favour of alternatives that make best use of an existing system (for example, gym equipment or computer software). There may have to be a delay in acquiring the ideal choice until a major expense can be justified.

Whether the starting point for the audit is the curriculum that the school wants to deliver, or the resources that it currently has available, the end result will be a list of resources that need to be acquired. As an audit process both approaches are essentially the same. Figure 8.1 presents and compares the trails.

Clearly the last part of the audit process has significant implications for the school – and how it manages its resource allocation process, in particular the degree of independence the subject leader has for the management of the subject's funding allocation. These financial considerations will be addressed in greater detail in the next chapter.

It is important to acknowledge that a subject leader cannot make resource acquisition decisions in isolation from the rest of the school. The bid for resource funding must be compatible with the curricular and financial priorities of the school. The way that one subject leader approaches the task of auditing and then bidding for resources will necessarily impact upon other subject leaders.

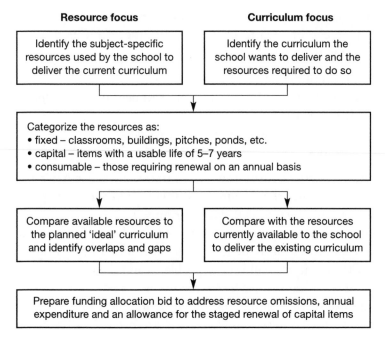

Figure 8.1 Resource and curriculum-focused audits
Source: Burton (2004: 184)

If the 'resource focused' approach to the audit is adopted, then, inevitably, a proportion of the resources identified are likely to be redundant to needs. However, they cannot and should not be abandoned without further consideration – some may have the potential to be adapted for alternative uses within school. Others may have the potential to be sold or donated to a non-school use (e.g. after-school club or playgroup).

ASK YOURSELF

♦ How aware am I of the full range of resources that my school has for my subject?
♦ Do I know where all of those resources are?
♦ To what extent do those resources meet the needs of the curriculum?

Maintaining resources

It is undeniable that one of the key tasks of the subject leader is to ensure that the resources are where they are meant to be and in an appropriate condition when a member of staff wants to use them. In recent years, the subject that has been vulnerable to maintenance issues has been ICT. The problems here can be seen to impact on all other subjects to some extent and fall into the following categories:

- The sturdiness of the resources.
- Technical competence (of both the subject leader and the teacher).
- Unrealistic expectations.
- Appropriateness of storage and retrieval systems.
- Incompatibilities.

Frequently, all factors conspire to ensure that the teacher has a frustrating time attempting to use the resource and this lack of success is passed on to the children whose learning is then compromised.

Resources used in primary schools need to be fit for purpose. They should be capable of surviving general use within an appropriate learning situation. Clearly misuse will lead to problems and the main cause of misuse is the lack of technical competence – the teacher is not fully aware or confident in the use of the equipment and so is unable to instruct the pupils correctly in its use or make simple repairs or corrections where necessary. This general lack of understanding of what the equipment is capable of is also likely to lead to unrealistic expectations being placed upon it, with the accompanying frustrations that it will release. Or it could simply be that it is stored in such a way that it is likely to lead to damage either in storage or as it is collected.

In almost all cases the answer to the problem is training. Where it is necessary to use equipment that is perhaps not as robust as one would like, teachers need to be made aware of this so that they can brief the pupils accordingly. It follows that teachers, or other staff responsible for the use of the equipment, need to be confident and competent in its use – training. This should then reduce the possibility of unreasonable expectations being made of it. Most storage problems are usually caused by not knowing how to do it properly rather than not having the proper facilities. Finally there may be compatibility problems – not everyone is able to use precisely the same resource. Different computers have different set-ups or software installed, there are different editions of the same textbooks or similar inconsistencies that lead to problems for insecure teachers and confusion for pupils. If at all possible resources should be acquired to ensure that there is consistency where appropriate and, where there are differences, the teacher is fully briefed.

Once the subject leader has fully inducted staff into the proper use and storage of the equipment, many of the problems should disappear. The task is then to ensure availability – consumables are ordered in appropriate quantities and checked in, resources are returned or retrieved from class-rooms, and they are checked over and stored ready for the next user.

ASK YOURSELF

- How confident am I in the use of all subject-specific resources in the school?
- How do I train staff in the use of new equipment and resources?
- Where do I go for support and help?

Subject leader as resource manager

By delegating resource management to subject leaders within the school there should be greater responsiveness to needs. By having one of the 'end users' responsible for resource acquisition and organization, there should be a closer bond with learning and teaching. Those with these responsibilities for resourcing the curriculum must be in tune with the overall aims and pri-orities of the school or college (Glover, 2000: 121). In some cases, particularly where the relative cost is high in proportion to other calls on funding within the school, there needs to be prior agreement with all key parties to establish the primacy of this focus.

Even where curriculum resource funding is devolved to the level of sub-ject leaders, the actual amounts are still relatively limited, the latest indications suggesting that this is in the region of 5 per cent of the overall school budget. Even so, for the devolution to be effective, school and sub-ject priorities for learning outcomes need to be harmonized by a clearly defined planning structure. Subject action planning should reflect the strate-gic priorities of the school. In order to plan for the following year's resource acquisitions, senior and middle managers need to be involved in an evaluat-ing of past use of resources. Glover (2000) found that many schools had difficulties in managing to co-ordinate learning priorities with resource pri-orities. In some cases it could be argued that, once educational priorities had been set, some schools found that the resources were already in exis-tence and just required organization, but this could not account for the majority of cases.

Given the management structure prevalent in many primary schools it is conceivable that subject leaders, who have had little or no input into setting the institutional priorities, are 'allocated some budgetary responsibility for implementing the consequences of these decisions' (Ainley and Bailey, 1997: 57). Headteachers can find themselves in similar circumstances, lacking ownership over the issues. The current emphasis on 'honey pot' management, where schools have to bid for funding which can only be used for strictly defined purposes, has meant that the priorities of individual schools can be distorted as government funding is made available.

Stoll and Fink acknowledge that 'it is neither manageable, possible nor a good use of teachers' time for everyone to be involved in the fine details of development planning' (1996: 63). What does need to be agreed and communicated is a clear vision for the school which encompasses the role that each subject will play in achieving the goals. Subject leaders should identify how their subject will contribute to the vision, and outline the resource implications. Where there are particular initiatives which the school wishes to prioritize and fund accordingly, an example being the greater use of learning technologies such as interactive whiteboards, then subject leaders should be actively seeking to enhance learning and teaching of their subject through this medium by identifying subject-specific activities and interactive resources. As was mentioned above during the discussion of the use of resource audits, it is often much more successful to build upon the resources that exist rather than approach the curriculum from a different direction requiring a significant resource input.

Organization of learning resources

Physical learning resources need to be organized and maintained so that classes have the resources they need for the modules that have been planned. This requires the consideration of accessibility. The more flexible and accommodating for teachers the resource management system is, the more carefully it needs to be controlled and maintained. While the level of security and certainly can be improved through the use of bureaucratic 'booking' systems, it may deter teachers from actually making use of the resources – an effective resource storage system is not necessarily a neat and tidy one, but an empty one indicates that the resources are actually being used around the school. However, a 'system' based upon complete open access might quickly lead to a situation where the resources are all too easily 'mislaid', their location or even continued existence being in doubt. The system must balance the cost of the resource against the desired ease of access to maximize proper usage – the loss or destruction of a paintbrush might be acceptable, but not a laptop. Teachers need to feel ownership of the resources if they are to be responsible for them – expectations need to be set and maintained across the school for all resources.

Acquiring new and replacement learning resources to enhance the delivery of the curriculum is a constant that all subject leaders must face. But stretching the budget as far as possible by exploring best deals and alternatives may lead to an increase in other costs – the subject leader's time. The whole point of obtaining 'value-for-money' resources is rendered ineffective if it leads to an excessive increase in time for the subject leader – are the savings that can be obtained 'worth' the effort? Given that, once a teacher is employed, his or her time is effectively 'free', some schools may feel that it is a perfectly reasonable expectation. It might be more effective to share the task between the subject leader, who identifies the resources required and potential alternatives, and a member of the administrative team who has experience as a 'buyer'.

ASK YOURSELF

- ◆ Is there specific policy on the storage of resources in the school?
- ◆ How are resource levels maintained?
- ◆ What proportion of the leadership role is spent on organizing the resources?

People as a resource

One of the most versatile and potentially most effective resources that subject leaders have available to work with are the people around them. The talents of individuals can be trained and honed to the benefit of both themselves and others. As with other resources, it is mainly a matter of identification, organization and effective application. Figure 8.2 identifies some of the key sources and their location relative to the focus of learning.

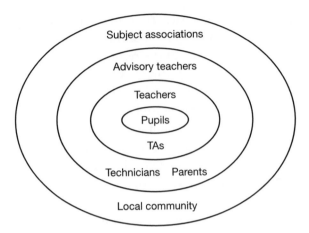

Figure 8.2 Key sources and their location

Pupils

Pupils are central to the learning process and so should be considered the central human resource. Through their enthusiasm and tangible evidence of their learning they are capable of inspiring others – perhaps through a display of their work in public areas of the school or by presentations in assembly or just by word of mouth in the playground, they can be wonderful ambassadors for your subject. Older children can gain self-esteem through being trained to take on additional responsibilities to develop the subject throughout the school. This might be achieved by supporting the learning of younger children in the subject – reading or playing mathematical games with younger children, demonstrating techniques in art or PE, etc. Alternatively, children can be trained to perform administrative tasks for the subject leader – such as acting as librarians; retrieving equipment from classrooms; checking the charge of batteries for science; etc. All these tasks offering real opportunities for pupils to apply their skills and knowledge to 'real' situations.

Teachers

While other teachers are likely to have subject leadership roles of their own, to a greater or lesser extent, it is well worth the time auditing the talents and experience that exist within the teaching staff – particularly as they relate to subjects. Some subjects can gain a mutual advantage by 'pairing off' and focusing on issues, skills or themes that are shared between them across the school. For example, music, drama, art and dance can regularly combine for a 'production', and PE, science and DT for a 'health education' week. By pooling resources and effort both the pupils and teachers can make significant gains from the process, which is fully compatible with the aims of the Primary Strategy (DfES, 2003). Resources can be developed to enhance the connectivity between subjects; this will apply particularly strongly to ICT as a format for learning in a range of subjects (either in terms of how generic software can be used within the subject, or the identification and use of subject-specific software or websites).

Given the nature of primary teachers and the balance of teaching staff in primary schools, there is a strong likelihood that there will be more than one specialist of a particular subject within the school (although they may be leading other subjects). Asking advice and comparing ideas can be of great benefit to the professional development of each concerned – as it is unlikely that all will have exactly the same strengths.

Teaching assistants (TAs)

It is the strongly expressed view of the government that 'teaching and learning can be strengthened by using the full potential of TAs' (DfEE, 1998: 55). Classroom-based TAs not only support pupils but also teachers in the delivery of the curriculum and the development of learning to 'improve the educational opportunities for the entire class' (Lorenz, 2001: 5). Some teachers use TAs in a non-teaching support role preparing materials and/or keeping detailed behaviour/assessment records of individual children. Some teachers, particularly in practical situations, prefer TAs to adopt more of a 'classroom management' role by providing 'an extra pair of eyes and ears' (Lorenz, 2001: 5) – particularly important for learning activities outside the classroom. The government has indicated that it is now 'common and desirable for teachers to allocate LSAs tasks that were once more often done by the teacher' (DfES, 2001: 8), such as is now commonly found with numeracy and literacy sessions and some ICT activities.

As with all human resource involvement in the learning process, the role of the TA can be made more effective with training and closer communication. The subject leader needs to make TAs more aware of the nature of the subject they are supporting so that they are able to see beyond the activities they are performing with the pupils, and specific objectives they are working to, to see the bigger picture of the subject development that the pupil is attempting. However, TAs need to be managed sensitively as research shows complaints that training 'had no impact on salary or career progression'

(Farrell *et al.*, 1999: 3). Indeed, teachers should receive training (Westwood Park, 2002) so that they can more effectively delegate these duties to TAs.

According to Mistry *et al.* (2004: 128), TAs 'need time to discuss with the appropriate members of teaching staff the monitoring and evaluating of various learning targets'. The communication does need to be clear and consistent as 'messages from different sources can be contradictory and confusing' (DfEE, 2000: 20).

Advisory teachers

It is all but impossible to know all that a subject leader needs to know about his or her subject when he or she also needs to maintain his or her standing in all other subjects of the curriculum. Similarly, it is very difficult to keep concurrent with all the developments in the subject – from the latest research on teaching methodology to the latest resources (and deals!). This is where the advisory teacher comes into play. As a 'full-time specialist' in a primary field they are much better placed to gather and disseminate information – ideally they will co-ordinate local groups where subject leaders are able to come together and benefit from each others' experience and knowledge.

Technicians

While they are quite a rare breed outside secondary schools their numbers are beginning to grow and their role develop. The significant growth of ICT has been a specific impetus behind the growth but other subjects are also beginning to benefit, especially with the new, more teaching-focused role of the TA. Even with the ICT technician alone, many subject leaders can be supported in their work through the use of ICT. Teachers who are lacking in confidence in the use of ICT can be supported by the technician so that all they need to concern themselves with is the subject content of the lesson. If the leader of art is attempting to encourage classes to explore the use of digital images, teachers might be more willing to attempt activities if they feel that they will be supported with the technical aspects.

Parents

Many parents have a significant and diverse range of skills and expertise that they would often be willing to share with the school (perhaps even as ICT technician!). An audit of parent skills may well reveal the existence of sports coaches, artists, musicians, town planners (geography), bakers, etc., all willing to share their expertise with the school in one way or another. This could be at the classroom level, working directly with the pupils, or in an advisory capacity to support and enhance the subject level support for the subject leader (e.g. local development maps from the town planner, and advice on how to interpret them). Usually all it will cost is a cup of tea (maybe some child care) and a small amount of time spent organizing the activity and performing a CRB check. Schooling should be a partnership activity and, if involvement in school can be encouraged so that parents and teachers can be working to the same goals, then everyone, especially the pupils, will benefit.

Local community

As with parents, there is a latent resource here waiting to be deployed. Not only do they bring with them the same range of skills and experience as parents, but they also provide the pupils with connectivity to their local community beyond their immediate family. Unlike with parents, though, the school does not necessarily have direct lines of communication with them so getting key members of the community involved – indeed, identifying who those 'key members' might be – calls for a greater effort on behalf of the school. There may be personal contacts that could be used (school staff or parents) but as with all adults invited into the school careful CRB checks need to be diplomatically made.

Local businesses are often a good source of resources (human or otherwise), particularly if they happen to be a major employer in the local community – it will always be good public relations for them to be seen supporting work in a school where their employees send their children. In a strictly subject-focused sense there may well be individuals working in the companies who are able to provide specific support for the subject leader.

Subject associations

Inevitably some subject associations cater for the primary phase better than others but all offer support for the subject leader through publications, websites and meetings and conferences. Organizations such as the Association for Science Education offer membership to primary schools who can then avail themselves of the support systems especially developed and resourced for the primary sector. Most will also provide the subject leader with a local support network where ideas can be discussed and common issues addressed; it will provide a means of disseminating good practice and communicating new developments.

- Whom can I look to for subject support both within and beyond the school?
- How do I make contact with potential experts outside the school?
- What is the school policy on bringing parents and members of the local community into the school?

Summary

A subject leader needs to be aware of his or her own strengths and weaknesses and know where to go to overcome the perceived deficiencies. Resources need to be carefully matched to the curriculum and staff fully trained in their use so that they can be employed for greatest impact, and those resources need to be made appropriately available. The subject leader needs to use ingenuity to identify and make most effective use of the resources that he or she has at the school's disposal – at all times being aware of the learning needs of the pupils and the educational direction of the school.

References

Ainley, P. and Bailey, B. (1997) *The Business of Learning: Staff and Student Experiences of Further Education in the 1999s.* London: Cassell.

Burton, N. (2004) 'Resource and environment management', in M. Brundrett and I. Terrell (eds) *Learning to Lead in the Secondary School.* London: RoutledgeFalmer.

DfEE (Department for Education and Employment) (1998) *Teachers: Meeting the Challenge of Change.* London: HMSO.

DfEE (Department for Education and Employment) (2000) *Working with Teaching Assistants: A Good Practice Guide.* London: HMSO.

DfES (Department for Education and Skills) (2001) *SEN Code of Practice.* Nottingham: DfES.

DFES (Department for Education and Skills) (2003) *Excellence and Enjoyment – a Strategy for Primary Schools.* London: HMSO (online at http://www.dfes.gov.uk/primarydocument/).

Farrell, P., Balshaw, M. and Polat, F. (1999) *The Management, Role and Training of Learning Support Assistants (RB161).* London: DfES (online at http://www.dfes.gov.uk/sen/documents/learning_support_assistants.htm).

Glover, D. (2000) 'Financial management and strategic planning', in M. Coleman and L. Anderson (eds) *Managing Finance and Resources in Education*. London: Paul Chapman Publishing.

Kelly, R. and Kedney, J. (1992) *Designing a College Accommodation Strategy. Mendip Papers* (MP053). Bristol: The Staff College.

Lorenz, S. (2001) *Effective In-class Support: The Management of Support Staff in Mainstream and Special Schools*. London: David Fulton.

Mistry, M., Burton, N. and Brundrett, M. (2004) 'Managing LSAs: an evaluation of the use of learning support assistants in an urban primary school', *School Leadership and Management*, 24: 125–37.

Murphy, M. (1994) 'Managing the use of space', in D. Warner and G. Kelly (eds) *Managing Educational Property: A Handbook for Schools, Colleges and Universities*. Buckingham: Society for Research into Higher Education and Open University Press.

Stoll, L. and Fink, D. (1996) *Changing our Schools*. Buckingham: Open University Press.

Westwood Park Community Primary (2002) *Successful System for the Management of Teaching Assistants* online at (http://www.teachernet.gov.uk/_doc/2925/WESTWOOD%20PARK%20COMMUNITY.final.doc).

Recommended reading

Anderson, L., Briggs, A. and Burton, N. (2001) *Managing Finance, Resources and Stakeholders in Education*. London: Paul Chapman Publishing.

Coleman, M. and Anderson, L. (2000) *Managing Finances and Resources in Education*. London: Paul Chapman Publishing.

Website

National Remodelling Team (2004) http://www.remodelling.org

9

Budgeting for the cost of learning resources

LEARNING OUTCOMES OF THIS CHAPTER

By the end of this chapter you should be able to:

- understand the key resource issues in starting a new initiative
- articulate the importance of finance as an educational resource
- analyse the budgetary process
- recognize the importance of effectiveness and efficiency and the ways in which decisions about the budget are taken

Starting a new initiative

Before embarking on any new initiative there are two questions to ask:

1 What will it cost to do it?
2 What will it cost *not* to do it?

All too often the first takes precedent as it provides the more tangible answer. However, this chapter will explore how the first can be accurately assessed and the importance of considering the answer to the second question.

As was learnt in the previous chapter, there is a wide range of resources that a primary school can call upon but none of them are truly free. While many have no obvious, direct monetary cost, their 'hidden' costs, particularly in terms of teacher time, need to be accounted for when decision are being taken.

Levacic (2000: 4) emphasizes the 'great responsibility in the hands of school ... managers to allocate resources to the best possible effect' – what limited financial resources there are must be used for greatest educational impact. In primary schools it is likely that, at least to some extent according to Burton (2004: 182), the 'subject specific cost of equipment and materials *will be* delegated to subject leaders'.

All educational activities within school are dependent upon the availability of financial resources. The subject leader is likely to have an impact on the effective management of financial resources influencing the quality of learning and teaching resources available for the subject. There is a need to gain the most educational benefit from the funding delegated to the subject. For this to be possible, subject leaders clearly need to possess or develop appropriate financial or budgetary management skills. Inevitably this will involve the ability to cope with a great deal of bureaucracy in order to ensure that funding is use wisely and appropriately in terms of ensuring that there is an appropriate system of resource acquisition, which may involve a lengthy process of developing and putting out tenders for bids.

With the devolution of financial management of many of the functions of state schools to the headteacher and board of governors, allied to various performance related targets, schools have adopted a 'goal orientation where funding is an enabler' (Palfreyman, 1991: 26). Since then there have been various pieces of research conducted, such as the one by Levacic and Glover (1998) examining the link 'between resource input and management process variables on the one hand and educational effectiveness measures on the other' (Levacic, 2000: 16). So far all research has shown that effective schools (using nationally determined standards) are those which employ rational decision-making processes to determine and allocate resources. According to Burton, a major goal for the school must be 'to transform the financial resources at the disposal of the school, into the most effective educational resources available' (2004: 169).

ASK YOURSELF

- ♦ How often is 'funding' used to determine decisions within the school?
- ♦ What is my awareness of the funding of my subject?

Finance as an educational resource

Caldwell and Spinks (1992) list finance as one among six forms of resource available to schools. They define 'financial resources' as the cash provided to a school for the purpose of purchasing tangible educational resources. This money is there to provide:

- *human resources*: teachers, teaching assistants (TAs), administrative staff and, arguably, to support unpaid volunteers; and
- *material resources*: buildings, equipment, furniture, books and teaching materials.

It is how well these two resources can be integrated that will be the major factor in determining the quality of the educational provision within the school. How well these resources are combined will be strongly effected by:

- *leadership*: power to make decisions (good, effective leaders command premium salaries);
- *professional development*: both the pedagogic knowledge and technology to deliver it have to be paid for; and
- *time*: as the saying goes, 'is money'!

Subject leaders with a proven track record of success are likely to be recruited or enticed to stay with an appropriate package of salary and benefits, involving additional increments on the standard teacher pay spine. Most professional development opportunities are made up of two costs – the cost of the input (the course or the consultant) and the cost of the time (supply teacher costs, or the cost of not doing an alternative activity). While teachers are salaried staff, rather than paid hourly, there are limits on the number of hours that they can reasonably be expected to work (from a physical if not moral stance) so their activities need to be carefully directed so as to employ their time to the greatest benefit to the children. As TAs are employed on an hourly rate, their deployment needs to be even more carefully managed to target learners and learning in specific subjects. The degree of delegation to subject leaders will vary from school to school but, while they may have control over the purchase of some types of resource and may have some influence on the professional development training that is bought into or the subject-focused deployment of TA hours, most decision will be made by a higher authority within the school. Whatever the level of responsibility that has been delegated, the subject leader will be a need to demonstrate the ability to manage a budget, at least as a means of informing the decision-making processes at school leadership levels.

The budgetary process

The budgetary cycle mirrors, in many respects, the teaching cycle (plan–teach–assess/evaluate–plan) in that a financial plan is put forward, agreed, then put into effect. It is then evaluated for impact and will inform the next round of planning. There are two ways in which to perceived the process: 'Budgeting and costing are two different approaches to determining the necessary funds for educational activities. Budgeting focuses on the allocation of available funds; costing on the funds that are required to allow certain educational activities to take place' (Burton, 1999: 129).

In effect, budgeting asks:

- What can we do with the funding we have available (to be as effective as possible with the resources we have got)?

While costing asks:

- What do we need to do what we want (to be as efficient as possible in achieving our goals)?

Both have particular strengths and work by perceiving the problem in different ways – with budgeting focusing on ensuring that available funding is not exceeded and costing focusing on the meeting of baseline objectives.

Why budget?

Burton presents four specific reasons for engaging in budgeting. Because:

1 resources are 'scarce' – you can't do everything that you want to;
2 you are accountable for the funding that you receive;
3 you want to ensure that the things you need to do are properly resourced; and
4 you want to plan ahead (in Anderson *et al.*, 2001: 27).

Burton continues: 'The budget is much more than a spreadsheet itemising income and expenditure under different section headings. It should be used as a means of expressing school or college aims and educational priorities in financial terms.' Expressly, the funding should be directly linked to the school's improvement plan to make the ideals of the plan a reality. A budget will demonstrate that funds are being directed appropriately in line with action-planning for each subject or initiative area. The information that the budget sheet is able to reveal can be a very effective decision-making tool for managers, providing a level of understanding that should ensure that the 'curriculum should drive the budget rather than the other way round' (Levacic, 1992: 26).

In every effective, well lead and well managed school, the budget will be used as an essential part of the annual cycle of planning and improvement, exerting control over both short and long-term decisions. The budget will need to be attached to and supported by decision-making procedures to determine how conflicting financial priorities are resolved, and the degree of consultation with subject leaders and other school staff that this will involve. The budget cannot be fixed, the environment in which schools

operate is far to dynamic for this to be a viable option, but should be sufficiently flexible to incorporate improvements and developments to the
school's situation by moving funds between headings and purposes.

Glover (2000), developing and rationalizing the earlier work of Levacic
(1992), concluded that the budgetary management of schools had three distinct purposes:

1 *Control*: making transparent the funding of the different educational priorities of the school.
2 *Accountability and stewardship*: to ensure that public funds can be clearly
  shown to have been used for appropriate educational purposes.
3 *Motivation*: to encourage ownership of the financial decision-making process through delegation of funding which, according to Caldwell and
  Spinks, 'encourages individual initiative when it is not possible to formulate a coherent and integrated organisational response' (1998: 199).

There are several ways in which a budget can be generated and presented.
While most schools will adopt a combination of approaches, the four discrete forms most commonly used are as follows:

1 Incremental budgeting.
2 Zero-based budgeting (also referred to as ZBB).
3 Priority-based budgeting (PBB) – also known as the programme planning,
  budgeting system (PPBS).
4 Formulaic budgeting.

Incremental

This approach employs the same overall pattern year on year, merely
making marginal or 'incremental' changes based on the global changes to
the annual budget. As an approach, there is much that can be said in favour
of it, most notably that it predictable and secure, offering no radical
changes to the funds that a subject leader is likely to find at his or her disposal. It is a rather mechanical process and so avoids the need for detailed
consultations with staff and the potential this may have for conflict (Davies,
1994: 348). However, the whole process is the product of a stable environment and, for most schools, that will not be the case. This inflexibility
suggests a number of potential problems that need to be resolved such as if,
in the past, a particular subject were to be given a disproportionate level of
funding, this disparity will be carried through into subsequent budgets. It is
unlikely that the system will be able to respond adequately to specific

changes in funding demands (e.g. an increase in the need for spending on ICT across the school). Finally, incremental budgeting makes the erroneous assumption that costs from all sources are rising at the same level.

Zero based

Rather like the 'curriculum-focused' approach to auditing, ZBB starts with a 'blank sheet', focusing on future needs rather than current expenditure. In many respects it is at the opposite end of the continuum from the incremental approach. Each budgetary cycle starts afresh so it should avoid any discrepancies that occurred in previous budgets. Fundamentally it is born of a dynamic process allowing new calls on funding and new initiative to be brought rapidly into the budgetary cycle with a decision being required to justify expenditure in each case. Clearly, having to evaluate the worthiness of every item of expenditure is a very time-consuming, and therefore costly, activity. Given that each budgetary cycle will begin without preconceptions, there could be problems achieving consistency of funding, year on year, for ongoing initiatives. It also tends to ignore the fact than many fixed costs (buildings, permanent staffing) are incremental in nature and don't require the level of financial interrogation expected by this approach.

Priority based

Priority-based budgeting focuses on prioritizing budgets to coincide with the educational goals of the school. This means that the budget is largely determined by the resources required to meet school or nationally determined priorities. It also ensure that the relative costs of means of working towards priority targets are also a key part of the educational debate within the school – funding informed decision-making. An alternative perspective on this is that the funding issues may drive the educational debate, with any radical changes, in the educational direction or focus of the school, leading to equally radical changes in funding.

Formulaic

A formulaic budget uses past expectations of the budgetary process and outcomes to produce a rational means of predicting future calls on funding. In this respect it is an amalgamation of the above processes offering a rational and defensible means of arriving at a budgetary position making a formal link between need and allocation. Being formulaic it is possible to build an ICT-based solution to producing a budget – or at least a first draft of it which provides a basis for discussion. However, this is what also makes it inflexible – the whole system is entirely dependent of the initial assumptions that have been built in and will need to be constantly checked and updated to ensure that the outcomes of the approach reflect the needs of reality.

Why calculate the cost?

Of alternative means of achieving the same, or equivalent, educational outcome, what is to be gained from choosing the most costly? Making educational decisions (such as which, of alternative reading schemes, to choose) without asking the cost could lead to a poor overall use of the funds available. In general, 'the activity of costing is best defined in terms of its purpose or outcomes' (Burton, 1999: 129). Unfortunately there is more than one way of determining cost:

● *Perceived costs*: the actual price paid against the hidden costs (in terms of time, general happiness, etc.).
● *Timescale*: the time over which the costs will have to be met.
● *Basis of cost*: total, average and marginal.
● *Identification of source*: direct and indirect costs (from Burton, 2004: 173).

In the past, when schools were simply given resources, rather than the funding to buy their own, it was not necessary to cost the decisions. As Kedney (1993: 1) asks, 'if provision is up and running, the quality is judged to be at least adequate, life is generally thought to be reasonable and will stay that way, so why bother with costing'? The delegation of funding to schools to make their own resource decisions has made them much more aware of the impact of their choices.

Not all costs can be accounted for simply by looking at the price sticker. There might well be other costs associated with it that are not taken into account initially – such as a new learning resource, which may have a relatively small price tag but as it will require a significant change to the approach to teaching and the rewriting of existing lesson plans, then staff may perceive its costs as being too high to contemplate. Every time a decision is made to use funds in a particular way, it means that those same funds can't be used for an alternative use. Both could have lead to an improvement in the quality of learning and teaching, but only one will be possible – an improvement in the resources for 'handwriting', say, may mean that the subject leader cannot afford the resources that would have lead to an improvement in the quality of teaching 'sentence structure'. One is the cost of the other in terms of the opportunity missed. 'Opportunity cost', as a concept, is 'concerned with the "value" of the best alternative use to which the resources can be put' (Kedney and Davies, 1994: 455). So even where a decision appears not to have a cost implication – the budget sheet stays the same for each of the alternatives – costs may still exist, and may indeed vary from individual to individual in terms of their perceptions of value:

> If it is decided to give the existing staff more non-contact time and to employ no more teachers then class sizes have to rise. There is no additional monetary cost, so no on-budget cost of increasing non-contact time. But there still is a cost: the educational benefits pupils would have experienced had they been taught in smaller classes (Levacic, 1993: 5).

Some costs, which may appear fixed, may actually be possible to alter, but only in the long term. For example, the contract for marking pitches may have been agreed for a five-year period, and so for that time it is a fixed annual cost for the PE leader. However, when the contract comes up for renewal, it will be possible to renegotiate. Some equipment can be purchased with a service agreement, so there is a one-off purchase price and an annual charge to maintenance. When comparing the alternatives, the total cost of the packages needs to be considered, not just the initial payment.

Some costs may remain 'fixed' for a particular range of activity then rise steeply beyond that. A five-user site licence for a piece of educational software is perfectly reasonable as long as no more than five PCs are making use of it at any one time. As soon as a sixth licence becomes necessary there will be an immediate doubling of costs as a further five-user licence has to be purchased. A year group leader may welcome additional pupils into the year group, as long as class sizes stay below or at the maximum 30. Up to that point each child brings in additional funding but costs very little extra to educate (the teacher and classroom are already 'paid for', and there may be sufficient slack in the system to provide the additional chair, table, etc.). But beyond 30 the school needs to consider the possibility of opening an additional classroom (assuming that they have empty room). The issue is then one of resourcing and staffing it – a considerably greater cost than the additional income received for the pupil.

The final element is cost attribution. If library books are funded from the English subject leader's budget, who buys the books to support the science curriculum? Who is responsible for the cost of shelving them? Who is responsible for organizing them? In many respects the collegiality shown in most primary schools is able to overcome such issues.

To give some idea of the practical application of such issues, consider how cost may be appropriately integrated into the educational decision-making process. Often similar resources can be obtained in different formats, and without cost information a decision made upon the best possible information will not be possible. Maths schemes might be available as textbooks, with the pupils writing in exercise books. Workbooks serve both purposes, or as a book of photocopyable masters that clearly would need to be copied, and so some means of storage of each pupil's completed work would be required. Once purchased, the textbooks might last five years, requiring just the ongoing cost of exercise books. Each pupil would require a workbook each year (or possibly more) but, while the photocopy master might last the same length of time as the textbooks, there will be a constant need to photocopy sheets with all the time and cost that involves. If, in all other terms, the educational value of each option is similar, then cost, over the expected life of the resources, can then be brought into the equation. However, it may be necessary to consider other factors, such as the security of future funding. If appropriate funding for the scheme cannot be ensured in future budgets, then buying the textbooks now (or sufficient workbooks for the same period) may be the prudent option. Another perspective might be that, in a one-class per year group school, the textbooks might appear to be the preferred option, but in a larger school (with three-classes per year groups) the photocopy master might appear much more cost effective as the only additional costs will be more copies of the same sheets.

ASK YOURSELF

- Do I take fully into account cost in making my resource decisions?
- Do I take recurring costs into my calculations?
- Have I ever acquired a resource and then found it too expensive to maintain?

Effectiveness and efficiency

> Let no one deride the word 'cheaper', there is no advantage in education being more expensive than it has to be (Knight, 1983: 15).

Within a resource-constrained school, a subject leader is surely duty bound either to find the least-cost method of achieving an agreed educational outcome or to achieve as much as possible with the resources that are available. Ofsted (2000) evaluates school effectiveness in terms of the following:

- The extent to which resources are used to maximize the achievement of the school's aims and objectives.
- The extent to which the school aligns its spending priorities with its educational priorities.
- The cost-effectiveness of programmes, procedures and practices.
- The quality of the educational outcomes which result.

Educational efficiency can be defined as being the 'cheapest means of accomplishing a defined objective' (Rumble, 1987: 74). The clarity with which the objectives of the educational activity can be stated becomes very important here as the targets need to be defined in some measurable way. All the perceptions of cost mentioned above will need to be taken into account to come to an understanding of 'cheapest': 'Cost-effectiveness … is concerned with selecting the least-cost alternative for securing the desired outcome' (Mortimore et al., 1994: 23).

Of the subject leader, Woodall suggests five key reasons for performing a cost-effective analysis prior to decision-making:

1 Testing the economic feasibility of proposals.
2 Projecting future educational costs.
3 Estimating the cost of alternative actions.
4 Comparing alternative means of achieving the same educational objectives.
5 Improving the efficiency of resource utilization to meet current goals (1987: 399).

A subject leader should be concerned with such matters because he or she should be striving to achieve as much as possible with the resources available or using as few of those resources that he or she needs to in order to achieve his or her educational goals. 'Cost effectiveness', according to Mortimore et al. (1994: 22), 'is highly desirable', because 'a school that uses its resources more cost-effectively … releases resources which can be used to promote further development' – they can achieve more for their pupils.

The school improvement plan will identify goals, from which the subject leader will identify supporting targets for the subject. By performing a cost-effectiveness analysis, not only will the subject leader be able to inform senior management of the affordability of the goal but also give information by which to determine the best way of achieving it. It is also then possible to go one step further and explore what might happen if the initiative or goal is not worked towards – what will be the cost of not doing it? Put simply, this analysis allows leaders to make better, more secure, decisions and to be able to justify courses of action.

ASK YOURSELF

- On what basis do I make my resource decisions?
- Do I consider alternative courses of action?
- How secure are my decisions/how convincing am I?

Making decisions

The tools developed above will provide the subject leader with the power to make effective rational choices and advise senior management on the most appropriate courses of action. This makes the assumption that decisions within schools are made on the basis of rational evaluation of the information presented. Coombs and Hallak (1987: 191) assert that 'good educational cost analysts can literally be worth their weight in gold', with the rider that they 'ask the right questions and arrive at responsible answers, and provided the decision makers understand the answers and take them seriously'. The subject leader must present the leadership team with evidence of the analysis and draw and justify the conclusions for them, but the decision still has to be made, and it is possible that further considerations will need to be taken into account.

Bush (2000) offers four models for financial decision-making within schools:

1 rational
2 collegial
3 political
4 ambiguous.

The 'rational model', according to Levacic (2000: 8), is defined as having 'clear aims and goals, which are pursued through formal structures and rational decision making'. Essentially it is a bureaucratic model based upon 'best practice'. Simkins questions just how realistic such a model is, claiming that in many schools 'goals are ambiguous, contested, or conflicting' (1986: 155), leading to analyses being made on the basis of incorrect or incomplete information and assumptions.

For more than 30 years (Campbell, 1985; Wallace, 1988) collegiality has been presented as the 'ideal' structure for primary schools. Based on the notion of the primary school staffed by professional teachers, each able to offer his or her own degree of expertise to the school to arrive at consensus decisions, the model has much to commend it. However the reality of the situation is the restriction of the time in which to make those decisions and the ability effectively to involve all staff in the process – including non-teachers. In attempts to maintain the illusion of corporate decision-making there is a pressure almost to enforce collegiality upon an increasingly weary staff. Bush (1995) and Simkins (1986) acknowledge this as a gradual slide towards a political decision-making process. Recently there have been attempts to revive the ethos of collegiality through giving more importance to the role of teams within the school, often based around year groups or key stages, which are perceived as being more appropriately sized units.

Politics is an almost inevitable consequence of a democratic decision-making process – even where the one person with the vote is the headteacher. Different individuals hold different perceptions of reality and they will often gravitate to those with similar outlooks to form groupings, often based to some extent on their position within the school. At least some of these groups will be likely to suffer from inertia and will try to maintain the status quo, while other groups will be looking to develop the school – but often in different, possibly conflicting, ways. Particular individuals or groups will probably find themselves in positions where they have significant influence over the decision-making process, holding views which conflict with the rational decision-making processes. Having the strongest argument will no longer be sufficient; it will be necessary to lobby groups and individuals who in turn will give their backing and influence the decisions of others.

The ambiguity model suggests a situation where the decision-making process lacks coherence or clarity, usually as the result of incoherent or masked goals for the school – if you don't know where you are going, then any direction will do. Internal lines of communication and management are fragmented and often circumvented with a general lack of transparency preventing the effective deployment of resources to meet educational priorities. The systems and structure employed by the bureaucracy will tend to hinder and inhibit good practice, with subject leaders often given responsibility to meet targets but not the powers to achieve them.

Summary

The goal of the subject leader in respect of the sound financial management of his or her subject 'must be the provision of high quality education within the constraints of the available budget' (Burton, 2004: 179). Working towards the goals of the school, the subject leader should bring to the senior management team fully costed and analysed options which will enable the school to progress using the development of the subject as the means. By identifying the decision-making processes at work within the school, the subject leader should be able to work within the system to bring about a desirable outcome, leaving both the school and the subject stronger.

References

Anderson, L., Briggs, A. and Burton, N. (2001) *Managing Finance, Resources and Stakeholders in Education*. London: Paul Chapman Publishing.

Burton, N. (1999) 'Efficient and effective staff deployment', in M. Brundrett (ed.) *Principles of School Leadership*. Dereham: Peter Francis Publishers.

Burton, N. (2004) 'Financial resource management', in M. Brundrett and I. Terrell (eds) *Learning to Lead in the Secondary School*. London: RoutledgeFalmer.

Bush, T. (1995) *Theories of Educational Management*. London: Paul Chapman Publishing.

Bush, T. (2000) 'Management styles: impact on finance and resources', in M. Coleman and L. Anderson (eds.) *Managing Finance and Resources in Education*. London: Paul Chapman Publishing.

Caldwell, B. and Spinks, J. (1992) *Leading the Self-managing School*. London: Falmer Press.

Caldwell, B. and Spinks, J. (1998) *Beyond the Self-managing School*. London: Falmer Press.

Campbell, R. (1985) *Developing the Primary School Curriculum*. London: Holt, Rinehart & Winston.

Coombs, P. and Hallak, J. (1987) *Cost Analysis in Education*. Baltimore, MD: Johns Hopkins University Press.

Davies, B. (1994) 'Models of decision making in resource allocation', in T. Bush and J. West-Burnham (eds) *The Principles of Educational Management*. London: Paul Chapman Publishing.

Glover, D. (2000) 'Financial management and strategic planning', in M. Coleman and L. Anderson (eds) *Managing Finance and Resources in Education*. London: Paul Chapman Publishing.

Kedney, R. (1993) 'Costing open and flexible learning', *OLS News*, Part 30.

Kedney, R. and Davies, T. (1994) 'Cost reduction and value for money', *Coombe Lodge Report*, 24: 441–524.

Knight, B. (1983) *Managing School Finance*. Oxford: Heinemann.

Levacic, R. (1992) 'Local management of schools: aims, scope and impact', *Educational Management and Administration*, 20: 16–29.

Levacic, R. (1993) 'Managing resources effectively', in *E326 Managing Schools: Challenge and Response*. Buckingham: Open University Press.

Levacic, R. (2000) 'Linking resources to learning outcomes', in M. Coleman and L. Anderson (eds) *Managing Finance and Resources in Education*. London: Paul Chapman Publishing.

Levacic, R. and Glover, D. (1998) 'The relationship between efficient resource management and school effectiveness: evidence from OFSTED secondary school inspections', *School Effectiveness and School Improvement*, 9: 95–122.

Mortimore, P. and Mortimore, J. with Thomas, H. (1994) *Managing Associate Staff: Innovation in Primary and Secondary Schools*. London: Paul Chapman Publishing.

Ofsted (2000) *Handbook for Inspecting Schools*. London: HMSO.

Palfreyman, D. (1991) 'The art of costing and the politics of pricing', *Promoting Education*, 2: 26–7.

Rumble, G. (1987) 'Why distance learning can be cheaper than conventional education', *Distance Learning*, v. 8/1: 72–94.

Simkins, T. (1986) 'Patronage, markets and collegiality: reflections on the allocation of finance in secondary schools', *Educational Management and Administration*, 14: 17–30.

Wallace, M. (1988) 'Towards a collegial approach to curriculum management in primary and middle schools', *School Organisation*, 8: 25–34.

Woodhall, M. (1987) 'Cost analysis in education', in G. Psacharopoulos (ed.) *Economics of Education: Research and Studies*. Oxford: Pergamon Press.

Recommended reading

Anderson, L., Briggs, A. and Burton, N. (2001) *Managing Finance, Resources and Stakeholders in Education*. London: Paul Chapman Publishing.

Coleman, M. and Anderson, L. (2000) *Managing Finance and Resources in Education*. London: Paul Chapman Publishing.

Website

Financial Management in Schools (2004) http://www.ncsl.gov.uk/mediastore/image2/fin_mgmt/index.htm

SECTION D

Leading and Motivating Colleagues and Pupils

10

Human resources: leading and managing to improve performance

LEARNING OUTCOMES OF THIS CHAPTER

By the end of this chapter you should be able to:

- recognize the key features of the 'learning organization'
- understand the importance of motivation and teamwork in leading staff
- recognize and articulate the implications of national initiatives such as performance management workforce remodelling

The learning organization

Following the work of writers such as Senge (1990), Hopkins *et al.* (1994; 1997) and Hadfield *et al.* (2002), the notion of 'the learning organization' has been a seminal influence on the aspirations of educational organizations in leading and managing staff. Within this notion leaders aspire to go beyond the concept of staff operating as effective autonomous practitioners to a systemic commitment to learning that permeates the whole of school life. As outlined in Chapter 4, more recently the notion of 'distributed leadership' or 'leadership from the middle' has emphasized the role of the subject leader and the department in contributing to the whole-school culture of improvement. At the core of these ideas remains the notion of well trained, carefully selected, reflective practitioners who take on leadership and management responsibilities according to their role and stage of development in order to work together for the good of the school and, most importantly, for the benefit of the children they teach.

The way that staff are judged has increasingly focused on league tables, benchmarking, target-setting, inspection, monitoring and so on. Recently the overall assessment of teacher quality has come to be bound up with performance management. Within this systematized process of teacher appraisal (in its widest sense) we must not lose sight of the fact that teachers are a very special and selected group who choose to spend their working days with young people, some of whom are known, even by their parents, to be difficult at times but, often unknowingly, are able to reward their teachers with success and delight (Brundrett and Terrell, 1994). This chapter outlines the overall goal of those involved in working with colleagues to enhance the human capacity of a school at the middle leadership level – that is, to create a learning organization. The chapter then goes on to outline the two seminal national initiatives that will impact on the way that staff are lead and managed: performance management and workforce remodelling.

Creating a learning organization through motivation and teamwork

The task of the middle manager, then, is to establish the culture of continuous improvement based upon the notion of a learning organization. Some of the characteristics of a learning department might be as follows:

- Shared values and beliefs.
- A focus on learning and learners.
- Moral purpose.
- Sharing.
- Collaboration.
- Co-operation.
- Inquiry.
- Reflection.
- Evaluation.
- Criticality.
- Involvement.
- Engagement in the department.
- Leadership from different people on different tasks.
- Good interpersonal relationships.
- Positive humour.
- Vision.
- A sense of direction.
- A sense of achievement.

- Having clear departmental policies and procedures (e.g. on the motivation and management of pupil behaviour, or marking and assessment).
- Having policies that are developed from school policies and the school improvement plan (Brundrett and Terrell, 2004).

The culture of the learning department is dominated by a relaxed atmosphere. There is a high level of discussion about learning and learners. The department has a common aim and a focus to their improvement strategies. New ideas are listened to positively and discussed. Decisions are made by consensus-building although there may have to be a degree of compromise and trialing of new ideas. Yet constructive analytical criticism is valued. The journey to this point may be long and complex, depending to a large extent on a variety of contextual factors over which the middle leader may have comparatively little control when first appointed. Crucially, these contextual factors will include the level of motivation of colleagues in the school or subject area, and the extent to which the staff work together as a team.

Everard *et al.* (2004: 25) argue that we should be concerned with the needs and potential of three parties when motivating people. These include the following:

1 The group which we are managing or in which we manage.
2 The individuals who make up that group.
3 The clients (pupils, parents, etc.) of the school.

These facts offer some advantage to the middle leader since teachers are generally motivated to work for the best outcomes for their pupils and any wise leader will attempt to 'bring staff on board' by sharing the development of goals that have clear relevance for the needs of children. Classical theories of motivation are often said to relate back to the work of Maslow (1943), who suggested that it was helpful to think of motivation being related to set of human needs which exist in a hierarchy that ascends through *physiological needs*, *security needs*, *social needs* and *ego needs*, to the need to for *self-actualization*. By this last concept Maslow was referring to the notion that we will remain discontented unless we exploit all our various talents and potential in a holisitic way that may include artistic and creative endeavour. Herzberg (1975) developed Malow's theories through experimentation and came to the conclusion that the things that make people dissatisfied are related to the job environment. Herzberg termed such environmental issues 'hygiene factors', and these include: organizational policies and administration; management; working conditions; interpersonal relationships; and money, status and security. Motivational theorists have been unanimous in giving a place to the need for a sense of achievement (Everard *et al.*, 2004: 31) but there are those who suggest that the intensity of this need varies from person to person (see, for instance, the work of McLelland, 1985), thus necessitating different strategies for different individuals. Everard *et al.* (2004: 35) thus suggest three basic rules that underlie the management of relationships:

1 We should remember to use motivators, such as people's need for achievement, recognition, responsibility, job interest, personal growth and advancement potential. This principle is as valid for the dinner lady as it is for teaching staff.
2 The relative intensity of psychological needs will vary greatly from person to person and over time. This means that we must be careful not to misjudge the needs of others whose attitudes may be caused by personal and social factors such as personal relationships and the home environment as well as professional competence and willingness.
3 We should try to suit our management behaviour to both the personality and the situation.

The relevance of these theoretical perspectives to school middle leaders is, to some extent, self-evident. Colleagues (and indeed children) require a clean, well resourced environment which offers the possibility of interpersonal and professional discussion with colleagues that leads to a sense of self-worth as an educator. If this can be developed to allow the individual to take some ownership of the organization of the school then, inevitably, he or she will have a far better chance of moving towards the kind of self-actualization that is the ultimate goal.

In essence the curriculum leader will be a team leader who will attempt to motivate the group of people who form his or her colleagues within the curriculum area he or she supervises or for the specific leadership tasks that are allocated to him or her. Such teams are the essential building blocks of the organization and the leader will wish to review their progress and strive for improvement in their implementation and development of their task or tasks. Belbin's work (1994) suggests that there is a need for a balance of team roles and uses an inventory to assess the balance between:

- implementers
- co-ordinators
- shapers

- innovators
- resource investigators
- monitor evaluators
- team workers
- completer finishers.

One complicating factor for the team leader in the primary school is that he or she rarely has the opportunity to choose his or her team because he or she is most likely to inherit or to be allocated the colleagues with whom the team leader will be required to work. It will, therefore, be difficult to apply Belbin's work with a team where, for example, everyone is naturally an 'innovator' and nobody is a 'completer finisher'. Nevertheless, the model is useful in analysing what the roles the team needs and what might need to be worked at to improve team performance. Moreover the serendipity of the skills that staff may bring to a team emphasizes the need for the team leader to spend time in team-building. Tuckman (1965) famously suggested that there are five stages in team development that include 'forming', 'storming', 'norming', 'reforming' and 'performing'. Everard *et al.* (2004: 171) reflect on Tuckman's work and suggest that the main steps in problem-solving and team-building are similar and include the following:

1 Define *what we are seeking to achieve* in the specific situation to solve the problem, including the criteria by which we shall judge success.
2 Identify *why* we are seeking to achieve this.
3 Generate *alternative means* of achieving this.
4 Decide *which means* to adopt.
5 *Act* on the decision.
6 *Review* successes and failures in order to improve performance.

We must remember, too, that the team of teachers will spend the vast majority of their time working as an individual in their own classroom (perhaps 21 hours per week), whereas working as a member of the team is either in small amounts of directed time, such as in team meetings, or is implicit and indirect (see Figure 10.1). The key for middle manager is to help staff to manage both those roles effectively to improve pupil achievement and to raise standards.

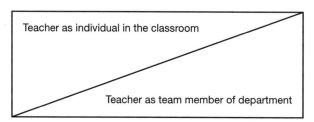

Figure 10.1 Teachers as individuals and as part of a team

Leask and Terrell (1997), borrowing the work of Fleishman and Harris (1972), Thomas (1976), Hersey and Blanchard (1982) and Blake and Mouton (1985), describe the tensions of leadership. They group two basic tensions between, on the one hand, concern for task, focusing on challenging, directing and assertive leadership behaviour, and, on the other, concern for people through supporting and co-operative behaviour. Again this model may be a useful tool for subject leaders to analyse team characteristics.

In a similar model, Cockman *et al.* (1992) remind us that in our concern for action plans and tasks to be achieved we often forget about the process issues. These include our interpersonal relationships, mutual respect, warmth and so on. Brundrett (1999) reviewed work by Morris and Murgatroyd (1986) and 'noted that management training should be based on communication skills, social skills, group processes and human relations' (Brundrett, 1999: 7).

Interpersonal relationships are the key factor in leadership and management at all levels, but especially at middle management. This area of work takes most time and energy. Facilitating individuals or groups of staff requires skill and professionalism, not least because so much takes place in time-pressured scenarios such as between lessons, at breaks or when pupils are around. Issues which you may need to work on with the team include performance and underperformance, disaffection, overenthusiasm, inexperience, stress, overwork and so on. People who share a common direction and sense of community can get where they are going quicker and easier on the thrust of another.

Brundrett and Terrell (2004) offer a number of key facts about leading people in schools which are applicable to those aspiring to lead in a secondary school. They are repeated here, slightly amended, in so far as they apply to middle leaders in primary schools.

Fact 1

It is important for a leader to provide clear vision and direction. It is even more important to ensure that all members of the school community share that vision and know what is expected of them in the drive to realize it. A good leader constantly seeks to ensure that all know what is expected of them. This is true of all leadership at all levels in the school.

Fact 2

People are not super-human. There will be times when people perform better than at others. There is no problem in asking for clarity and additional support. We should not operate a blame culture, which makes people ashamed to seek help and advice. Good leaders provide systems of support for all members of staff through well structured line management systems and mentoring and buddy systems.

Fact 3

A good leader recognizes the strengths and skills of all members of the department and school community and plays to those. This is vital when allocating tasks to colleagues. Staff who do not appear to be performing well in one role of responsibility may not be suited to that particular role. We should not seek to blame, to write them off immediately and begin capability procedures. It may be that they can perform to a high standard in a different capacity within the school. For example, a good head of department will not necessarily make a good head of year. It is also important to allow people the opportunity to take a lead in areas where they have the superior knowledge and skill. The leader is not the fount of all knowledge. He or she does not know everything about everything nor should he or she be expected to. The person responsible for whole-school assessment should be the expert in that field and lead the staff forward. The person responsible for PSHE should lead on that and so on. Poor leaders fear to relinquish the lead position.

Fact 4

Praise and encouragement, always seeking to promote the positive, help people to feel a sense of achievement. A good leader ensures that individual progress in terms of teacher performance and welfare is regularly checked upon. There are several ways, including the line management and mentoring systems mentioned earlier. Half-hour, fortnightly meetings with co-ordinators and heads of year or department (for instance, infant/junior) can help as will letting staff know when you will be available for people to drop in, following up on information received from other people and checking out clues picked up from people's body language. Nothing is worse than allowing people to dwell on something and build it all out of proportion when it may be a misunderstanding. Check it out!

Fact 5

In the current climate we are far too keen to seek to apportion blame and to claim that it's not our fault. Knowing whom to blame is not much of an insight into how to make things better. If someone is not performing it is up to the manager to find out why before taking action. Some teachers get very stressed out and it has become taboo to admit to suffering from stress. However, early intervention can prevent long-term damage to the teacher and, therefore, helps the school. We should seek to problem solve together for the benefit of the whole school community.

Fact 6

As a leader and manager you have a key role in developing and building the common direction. This partly involves building a joint vision but also a sense of community. Community spirit and being part of a common venture are key. This involves building an attachment and identity with the team efforts. Communicating regularly is vital to this. Stoll and Fink (1996) developed the notion of 'invitational leadership' involving communicating to people that they are valued, trusted and responsible.

The notion of leading others to take leadership roles is an interesting concept, but clearly only attained by some. Empowering staff is also about creating positive opportunities for people to develop. Staff may feel balked by leaders who do not wish for their leadership territory to be invaded.

ASK YOURSELF

- ◆ Have you spoken to every member of staff you lead today, or this week?
- ◆ What did you say?
- ◆ Was this personal or professional discussion or a mixture of the two?
- ◆ How did you relate to your colleague? For instance, did you feel that you both ended the discussion feeling valued and motivated?

A major role of the subject leader is in the leadership of staff development in the subject. However, it has long been understood that curriculum development, professional development and personal development are intertwined aspects of this role. The development of thinking skills activities in history, for example, requires some changes in curriculum and teaching methods. It also involves changes in the way people see themselves as teachers. It may affect the teacher's self-perception and the way he or she might see him or herself as a teacher. The kind of teacher he or she wants to be. One would hope that the experience of change is one of growth and that the teacher gains confidence and motivation.

The staff development role takes place in both formal and informal environments, and activities may include the following:

- Leading department and subject discussions.
- Introducing new ideas and approaches to teaching.
- Supporting staff developing effective teaching in the subject.
- Mentoring staff.
- Acting as a leading consultant.
- Observing classrooms and discussing those observations.
- Coaching staff in specific techniques.
- Development planning with the department.
- Establishing practitioner research and development.
- Leading in-service activities.
- Being involved in 'performance management'.

Coaching, mentoring and acting as an internal consultant to staff are different roles. Coaching tends to be more like acting as, say, an athletics trainer does and concerned with perfecting agreed techniques or skills. The coach observes and provides techniques to improve performance, frequently giving feedback on progress. Mentoring tends to be more advisory and acting in a counselling role. It explores feeling and problems more. Negotiating agreed solutions to problems is a central part of mentoring. Consultancy can span both coaching and mentoring (Leask and Terrell, 1997). Leask and Terrell, (1997), following Cockman et al. (1992), recommend a variety of approaches as an internal consultant including balancing being 'prescriptive' with being 'catalytic'. This involves using statements such as 'You need to' and 'You have to', as well as a more exploratory approach such as 'Have you tried?', 'What happens if?' 'What are your options?' These approaches deal with emotions with questions such as 'How does it feel when?', as well as confronting what people say and do.

Case study

Alex moved to his current large primary school two years ago to co-ordinate science and has been in teaching a total of four years following a previous career as a lab technician in a hospital. Since taking on his current role he has recognized that, while his enthusiasm for science can have a major impact on the children that he directly teaches, the quality of science provision across the school as a whole is not as good as he hoped it would be. Initially, he decided to operate by taking science lessons throughout Key Stage 2, but found that this had a detrimental effect on his own class and had to abandon the approach. Following discussions with a more experienced science co-ordinator from a local school he was helped to realize that his lack of organizational skills beyond his own classroom were what was holding back progress in science in the school. Rather than attempting to do it all himself, he began by more formally supporting the work of other teachers. When given classroom release time he began to use a mixture of exemplar lessons to demonstrate techniques to other teachers and coaching of teachers during science lessons. He found that by focusing his enthusiasm on the teachers, especially during training days, rather than the children in their classes, he was beginning to have a more lasting impact on the quality of science teaching and learning. By offering further and more formal support for planning and resource acquisition, senior management were also able to identify greater confidence in the teaching of science across the school.

Case study

Louise had been working in the school that she had been appointed to as a newly qualified teacher some 14 years previously and in that time had avoided taking on any significant curricular responsibility. However, staff, parents and pupils generally regarded her as one of the most effective and caring teachers in the school. With the arrival of a new headteacher she was placed under increasing pressure to accept greater responsibility for management within the school. Once it was clear that the pressure was having an adverse effect on her teaching a meeting was held to find the best way forward. Louise was encouraged to recognize how her nurturing and supporting approach to the children also spilled over into the way she worked with trainee teachers. Through recognizing how a classroom strength had a much wider impact within the school, she was able to acknowledge that she did have the skills to take on a management role within the school. First, by becoming the school mentor for work with initial teacher training students, she was able to build her own confidence and realize that many of the bureaucratic tasks that she performed in the class with the children (assessing, reporting, recording) were fundamentally the same as the way she needed to operate with the trainees, providing them with the opportunities and encouragement to succeed. With this success in place, the head now feels in a position to encourage and support her in taking a further step, with Louise becoming the NQT mentor and organizing induction for all new members of staff, with a view to her taking on the staff training portfolio within the next 18 months. As an excellent 'all-round' teacher, Louise did not have the confidence in any one particular curriculum area, but her success with 'people-centred' issues required a different management development route to be considered.

Overall a middle leader will need to employ a wide variety of skills in order to develop a team of colleagues. This is a complex task made all the more difficult by the limited amount of time that such a team can spend together and the even more limited resources that a middle leader will have at his or her disposal. It will be essential that the middle leader works closely with the senior management team and especially that the headteacher is consulted and informed about what is going on as the individual and team strive to improve the school. It is only through such consultative and inclusive practices that there is the possibility of building towards the learning organization.

Performance management and the curriculum leader

It became a statutory requirement for all maintained school in England and Wales, in September 2000, to review their existing arrangements for the monitoring and appraisal of staff and to agree a new performance management policy. Every school had to have a performance management policy, agreed by the governing body, by 31 December 2000: 'We want to improve school performance by developing the effectiveness of teachers, both as individuals and teams. The evidence is that standards rise when schools and individual teachers are clear about what they expect pupils to achieve. That is why performance management is important' (DfEE, 2001: 2).

Schools have always managed performance, and often effectively. However, these requirements were enforced to make the systems more formalized, to replace the, shall we say, ineffective, poorly thought-of and failing teacher appraisal schemes of the 1980s and 1990s and to promote further the notion of performance-related pay, a thing that has been and still is met with very mixed feelings and, most commonly, rejection on the part of the teaching unions. The DfEE Performance Management Framework states: 'Performance management demonstrates schools' commitment to develop all teachers effectively to ensure job satisfaction, high levels of expertise and progression of staff in their chosen profession' (DfEE, 2000: 1).

Hartle *et al.* (2001: 3) offers us the following definition of performance management: 'A process that links teachers, support staff and their respective roles to the success of pupils and the school.' Most schools have developed a performance management policy, using available models and following wide consultation with staff in the school, and middle managers often play a key role in helping to develop such policies. Schools who followed this route adopted a sensible approach as middle managers, referred to by the DfEE as 'team leaders', have a crucial part to play in this process.

The DfEE guidelines were keen to emphasize some important issues. The performance management cycle is ongoing – planning, monitoring and reviewing. It is intended to bring together the teacher's priorities, the needs of the pupils and the teacher's professional and personal priorities with the school improvement plan therefore becoming an integral part of the school's culture. The role of the team leader is to agree the focus for the teacher's work at the start of the performance management cycle. They have to ensure that each teacher understands what his or her objectives are and that they are related to the school improvement plan. They need to ensure that teachers are in a position to achieve them. They need to ensure that all teachers understand how and when these objectives are likely to be reviewed. This includes the issue of evidence. What will they be looking for to show that an objective has been achieved? This requires them to have knowledge and understanding of such benchmarking information as the school's PANDA report, other school performance data and prior attainment of pupils.

An effective manager pays constant attention to progress throughout the year. This requires a great deal of time and commitment from the team leader. They have to ensure that they themselves fully understand the school's policy and then pass that on to staff. They have to encourage and support staff in meeting their objectives. They have to monitor staff performance, including observing lessons.

The team leader then has to review the performance of the teacher. The intention is that the teacher and the team leader can reflect upon the teacher's performance in a structured way. The team leader needs to take into account the position of the teacher within the school (e.g. is he or she an

NQT or an AST?). It then requires them to make a professional judgement about their performance. This is doubly crucial, as there may well be money involved: 'The outcomes of the performance review will be used to inform pay decisions, for example for awarding double performance increments for outstanding performance up to the performance threshold' (DfEE, 2000: 9). This puts a great deal of pressure on team leaders. In addition, performance threshold assessment is intended to work alongside performance management. It is worth while referring to threshold assessments at this point because some of the same principles apply. The *School Teachers' Pay and Conditions* document places a duty on teachers who manage staff to 'assist, on request, the head or the assessor to carry out threshold assessments of the teachers they manage ... such a manager could be a head of department' (DfES, 2002: 19). Judgements are made on eight standards:

- Knowledge and understanding.
- Teaching and assessment (three standards – planning lessons, classroom management and monitoring progress).
- Pupil progress.
- Wider professional effectiveness (two standards – personal development and school development).
- Professional characteristics.

This means that as a middle manager you have to deal with a number of issues that may not be comfortable because of formality replacing informality and because the decision to increase the pay of certain staff is partly in your hands. This is, needless to say, very emotive issue.

ASK YOURSELF

- ◆ Do you have a copy of your school's current performance management policy?
- ◆ Do you understand how it operates? If not, ask your line manger to go through it with you.
- ◆ Do staff in your department have one?
- ◆ Have you received training in holding a performance management interview?
- ◆ What experience have you had in classroom observation?
- ◆ Do all the staff in your department have clear job descriptions? If not, review and revise.
- ◆ In making a professional judgement, what is your evidence base? (After DfEE, 1998).

The stages of the performance management cycle are:

1 planning
2 monitoring progress
3 review.

The planning phase requires a record to be kept of four objectives covering pupils progress and professional practice. Objectives would normally cover such things as:

- lesson preparation
- subject knowledge
- teaching methods
- communication and motivation
- discipline
- marking and assessment
- use of homework
- classroom organization
- implementation of school policies
- additional responsibilities.

Classroom observation and the collection of other evidence are required in the monitoring progress phase. This might involve a number of other exercises such as:

- scrutiny of pupil work;
- collecting information from students; and
- analysis of lesson plans and documentation.

Performance management can be unobtrusive within positive relationships and a culture of inquiry and development, since much of the information and process is a normal part of improvement. Balancing the formal requirement, the professional entitlement and the informal process of team achievement is a major problem for the middle manager.

In operationalizing the performance pay model we must remember that its prime purpose is considered to be the recruitment, retention and motivation of the workforce based on an assumption that the best-quality employees are attracted to organizations where ability is recognized and rewarded. Wragg and Wragg (2002) have, however, revealed that salary is only one of many factors that influence the decision as to whether or not to enter the profession. Ultimately it may be that the additional financial incentives embodied in performance pay will be insufficient as a mechanism to motivate teachers and a greater concentration on the interpersonal and social relationships in schools will be required (Wragg *et al.*, 2004: 183). Talented leaders at all levels in schools will recognize this fact and will seek to employ performance management within the framework of a much more sophisticated framework of staff development.

Workforce remodelling

A national agreement between government, employers and school workforce unions was signed on 15 January 2003 (ATL *et al.*, 2003) which promised joint action, designed to help every school across the country to raise standards and tackle workload issues. The National Agreement on Raising Standards and Tackling Workload states that:

> To achieve the demands of the next phase in raising standards, teachers will need to take a more differentiated approach to the needs of their pupils. And yet they are already doing too much of their planning, preparation and assessment (PPA) at evenings and weekends, and in isolation from each other. While this cannot be changed overnight, the Agreement marks a turning point in carving out some guaranteed PPA time during the normal school day.

Under the terms of the agreement, all teachers in maintained schools, who are employed under the *School Teachers' Pay and Conditions* document, must be allocated a guaranteed minimum of 10 per cent of their timetabled teaching time as PPA. This includes unqualified teachers and members of the leadership group with a teaching commitment. The purpose of guaranteed PPA time is to enable teachers to raise standards through a combination of individual or collaborative professional activity. It is also intended to improve teachers' work–life balance. It is suggested that the creation and implementation of a sustainable staffing plan, to include the provision of guaranteed PPA, can be seen as a three-step process: developing strategies; integrating strategies into the school timetable; and planning the evolution of strategies over time as an integral part of the school development plan, as represented in Figure 10.2.

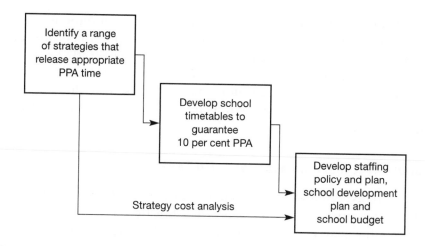

Figure 10.2 Stages in the creation and implementation of a sustainable staffing plan
Source DfES (2005: 2)
Crown copyright material is reproduced with the permission of the Controller of HMSO and the Queen's Printer for Scotland.

Schools are encouraged ask key questions of activities that take place, such as: is it necessary? Should we be doing this task? Why are we doing this task? Is the person carrying out the task the most appropriate person to be doing it? Can it be transferred to another person? An evaluation should also be made as to whether necessary tasks, such as pastoral activities, which are currently included as part of timetabled teaching time, could be moved to be outside timetabled teaching time but within the normal school session time. A persuasive commitment to amending the work–life balance of staff is evidenced in the documentation, and school leaders have been exhorted to examine their traditional rationale and schema for the kinds of interactions that take place in order to ensure that teachers are freed from unnecessary and inappropriate burdens:

> It is imperative that care is taken to ensure that this does not increase overall teacher workload. If activities, or aspects of activities, are not a good use of teachers' time, they should be reallocated to a more appropriate person – for example, a member of support staff – reduced or even, when appropriate, discarded. It is vital that schools make a thorough assessment of any change to ensure that their quality of care and teaching and learning is maintained and/or enhanced. Schools should also have regard to the overall work/life balance of all staff (DfES, 2005: 5).

The kinds of activities it is suggested that can potentially be reallocated, reduced or discarded, include administration; pastoral care; training and coaching; parent liaison; and working with other organizations. This list immediately reveals the amplitude of the challenge facing schools because it encompasses a variety of complex tasks that have consistently been undertaken by teachers who employ all their experience, training and expertise to accomplish them. The suggestion is that such tasks can alternatively be accomplished by non-teaching staff as part of an overall strategy that will employ the following groups.

Higher-level teaching assistants (HLTAs)

HLTAs are expected to make a significant contribution to teaching and learning activities – working under the direction and supervision of a teacher – for example, contributing to the planning and preparation of lessons, monitoring and assessing pupil participation and progress, providing feedback to teachers and giving constructive support to pupils as they learn, and working with individuals, small groups and whole classes where the assigned teacher is not present.

Instructors

A person with 'specialist qualifications or experience or both' can deliver specified work, provided the LEA and/or school governing body are satisfied that he or she has the relevant qualification or experience, or both. They are contractually entitled to PPA time for the timetabled teaching they do.

Specialist staff

Specialist staff may already be employed by the school or can be brought in from outside. They may be existing support staff as long as they have qualifications or experience in their speciality – for example, a member of support staff who is a dancer or a native French speaker. Other examples include sports coaches and local business people (DfES, 2005: 5).

The problematic element here is the extent to which sufficient appropriately skilled additional members of staff can be employed who fit within the categories defined above and whether, even if they can be found, they will have all the necessary attributes and complex skills to supervise and to educate children. The workforce remodelling agreement holds out the possibility that school-level restructuring can enhance the work–life balance of staff and enable teachers to focus on the tasks that are central to their professional role in enhancing learning. There are, however, a set of concerns surrounding the development of PPA time that will have to be faced as the initiative comes into force. There are three areas that are of particular concern. First, the cost of resourcing the reforms that are required is challenging, and although the government suggest that they have provided sufficient funding to implement the reform many staff, particularly headteachers, feel that there is insufficient funding to undertake the major change that is required in the ways that schools function. Secondly, in a connected issue, the role of support staff has come under scrutiny with questions being raised about the suitability of non-teachers to supervise whole-class groups of children. Thirdly, questions remain as to whether the work–life balance of teachers really will be improved. In the initial stages of the reform there is evidence that the workload of headteachers has actually been increased because of the additional effort required to implement the agreement at the local level and, although there may be a reduction in the workload of teachers, they still report that they are working over 50 hours per week (Slater and Stewart, 2004). It is undoubted that middle leaders will need to work with colleagues, old and new, teachers and non-teachers, to discuss, articulate and define the learning activities that pupils will undertake under this new model of the school workforce.

ASK YOURSELF

- In which tasks and activities in the area of the curriculum that I am responsible for are there core activities that must be undertaken by teaching staff?
- What activities are there that could be undertaken by other types of staff?
- What are the key skills and attributes that I would look for in non-teaching staff?

Summary

As stated at the start of this chapter, the overall goal in schools is to create a well trained, highly motivated staff who, together with other stakeholders, form a learning organization. The way that this overall goal is to be met is increasingly dominated by national strategies such as performance management and workforce remodelling. Governmental attempts to increase teachers' pay and to enhance the work–life balance are, of course, to be welcomed but such strategies can come at a price and that price is an ever-increasing central control on the role, remit and rights of teachers. Such central initiatives inevitably erode the professional autonomy of teachers who are monitored, evaluated and directed in their work. Schools have, however, been courageous and creative in the ways that they have interpreted the myriad of initiatives that are placed upon them and middle leaders in schools will have an increasing role in leading and managing the changes brought about by new ways of working. This is likely to be especially the case with workforce remodelling where curriculum co-ordinators will need to work with all staff to envision new systems of curriculum organization that enable the school to continue to offer the best possible learning experiences to children in a period of dramatic change. It is to this topic that the next chapters turns.

References

ATL, DfES, GMB, NAHT, NASUWT, NEOST, PAT, SHA, TGWU, UNISON and WAG (2003) *Raising Standards and Tackling Workload: A National Agreement*. London: DfES.

Belbin, M. (1994) *Team Roles at Work*. San Diego, CA: Pfeiffer.

Blake, R.R. and Mouton, J.S. (1985) *The Managerial Grid*. Houston, TX: Gulf Publishing.

Brundrett, M. (1999) *Principles of School Leadership*. Dereham: Peter Francis Publishers.

Brundrett, M. and Terrell, I. (eds) (2004) *Learning to Lead in the Secondary School: Becoming and Effective Head of Department*. London: RoutledgeFalmer.

Cockman, P., Evans, B. and Reynolds, P. (1992) *Client Centred Consultancy*. Maidenhead: McGraw-Hill.

Collarbone, P., (2002) *Reflections on Headship* (online at http://www.ncsl.org.uk/index.cfm?pageid=ev_auth_collarbone).

DfEE (1998) *Teachers Meeting the Challenge of Change*. London: HMSO.

DfEE (2000) *Circular 0051/2000: Performance Management in Schools*. London: DfEE.

DfEE (2001) *Performance Management in Schools: Model Performance Management Policy*. London: DfEE.

DfES (2002) *Performance Management: Threshold Guidance*. London: DfES.

DfES (2005) *Time for Standards: Transforming the School Workforce. Planning, Preparation and Assessment Strategies: Overview and Toolkit*. London: DfES.

Everard, K.B., Morris, G. and Wilson, I. (2004) *Effective School Management* (4th edn). London: Paul Chapman Publishing.

Fleishman, E.A. and Harris, E.F. (1972) 'Patterns of leadership behaviour related to employee behaviour', *Personnel Psychology*, 15: 43–56.

Hadfield, M., Chapman, C., Curryer, I. and Barrett, P. (2002) *Building Capacity. Developing your School*. Nottingham: NCSL.

Hartle, F., Baker, C. and Everall, K. (2001) *Getting the Best out of Performance Management in your School*. London: Kogan Page.

Hersey, P. and Blanchard, K. (1982) *Management of Organisational Behavior*. Englewood Cliffs, NJ: Prentice Hall.

Herzberg, F. (1975) *Work and the Nature of Man*. Reading, MA: Crosby Lockwood.

Hopkins, D., Ainscow, M. and West, M. (1994) *School Improvement in an Era of Change*. London: Cassell.

Leask, M. and Terrell, I. (1997) *Development Planning and School Improvement for Middle Managers*. London: Kogan Page.

Maslow, A.H. (1943) 'A theory of human motivation', *Psychological Review*, 50: 370–96.

McLelland, D.C. (1985) *The Achieving Society*. London: Simon & Schuster.

Morris, G. and Murgatroyd, S. (1986) 'Mangement for diverse futures: the task of school management in an uncertain future', *School Organisation*, 6: 46–63.

Senge, P. (1990) *The Fifth Discipline*. London: Century Business.

Slater, J. and Stewart, W. (2004) 'Reforms failing to reduce workload', *The Times Educational Supplement*, 19 November: 1.

Stoll, L. and Fink, D. (1996) *Changing our Schools*. Buckingham: Open University Press.

Thomas, K.W. (1976) 'Conflict and conflict management', in M. Dunnette (ed.) *Handbook of Industrial Management Psychology*. Skokie, IL: Rand McNally.

Tuckman, B.W. (1965) 'Development sequences in small groups', *Psychological Bulletin*, 63: 384–99.

Wragg, C.M. and Wragg, E.C. (2002) 'Staying power', *Managing Schools Today*, October: 32–5.

Wragg, E.C., Haynes, G.S., Wragg, C.M. and Chamberlin, R.P. (2004) *Performance Pay for Teachers: The Experiences of Heads and Teachers*. London: RoutledgeFalmer.

Recommended reading

Bush, T. and Middlewood, D. (eds) (2005) *Managing People in Education.* London: Paul Chapman Publishing.

Cockman, P., Evans, B. and Reynolds, P. (1992) *Client Centred Consultancy.* Maidenhead: McGraw-Hill.

Williams, J. (2002) *Professional Leadership in Schools: Effective Middle Management and Subject Leadership.* London: Kogan Page.

Website

National Remodelling team website (http://www.remodelling.org/what_na. php; http://www.belbin.info/).

11

Curriculum leadership

LEARNING OUTCOMES OF THIS CHAPTER

By the end of this chapter you should be able to:

- articulate the key ideas in the co-constructivist model of the curriculum
- lead and manage for creativity in the curriculum
- describe and enact some of the key strategies in the personalized learning agenda

The role of schools and the movement from teaching to learning

Schools serve a variety of functions including the socialization of children, cultural reproduction of societal norms and values, cultural change and development, opportunities for gainful employment by teaching and other staff, and places of refuge and security for children in challenging circumstances. All these are important reasons why schools exist, and this multifaceted set of roles is one of the reasons why schools are complex organizations which give rise to contestation and discussion. One reason why schools exist is, however, a matter of general agreement – schools are there to enable, encourage and facilitate learning. We must remember though that learning is itself a problematic concept and, as Middlewood and Burton (2001: ix) point out, for all the period up to the latter part of the twentieth century it was far more common to talk about teaching than learning. These two concepts, teaching and learning, are of course inexorably linked but different and the gradual movement towards the adoption of the term 'learning' to describe what goes on in schools is underpinned by a commitment to a set of notions about the ownership of the curriculum which have great importance for the role of both teacher and learner that will be analysed later in this chapter.

This shift in the way many conceive learning in schools is underpinned by a number of developments during the last 20 years that have increased our understanding of what it means to be a learner:

- Increasing discoveries about how the brain works.
- Ideas about 'multiple intelligences' (see, for instance, Gardner, 1993).
- The recognition of the importance of 'emotional intelligence' (Goleman, 1996).
- The realization that different pupils have different learning styles (such as the visual, auditory, kinaesthetic).
- The influence of rapidly evolving ICT.
- The interest in schools being learning organizations (Middlewood and Burton, 2001: x).

The extent to which these discoveries, ideas and developments will influence learning and teaching in the long term has to be played out. Some items on the list, such as the notion of multiple intelligences, may turn out to have only passing influence on schools; others, such as ICT, are almost certain to have a continuing and ever more important impact on both the physical and pedagogical environments of schools. What all these items have in common is the fact that they underpin a commitment to the importance of the individual in the learning and teaching situation. If people have different learning styles or approaches then it simply makes sense that we need to take account of the needs of the individual learner when planning his or her learning opportunities. One of the challenges of this chapter, and any discussion of learning, is that the word learning has very different connotations for different people (Carnell and Lodge, 2005: 208). For instance, people might conceive of learning as acquiring more knowledge; memorizing or reproducing facts; applying facts or procedures; understanding; seeing something in a different way; or changing as a person (Marton *et al.*, 1993).

Models of the curriculum and the learning that underpins it

In the broadest sense it is these learning opportunities, however we conceive them, that make up what we term 'the curriculum' which can, in turn, be defined as 'the educative process as a whole' or, much more narrowly, as 'the syllabus, a scheme of work, or simple subjects' (Richmond, 1971: 87). In this chapter we have chosen to employ this term, 'curriculum', since it remains in common parlance in schools, in governmental publications and in the educational community at large, but we may equally have stuck to the term 'learning' without ever employing the overarching concept of curriculum. Carnell and Lodge (2005: 212–14; see also Silcock and Brundrett, 2002) identify three models of learning that underpin the curriculum:

1 *Reception model*: where the learner is a passive recipient of knowledge transmitted by the teacher.
2 *Constructivist model*: where learners actively construct knowledge through such activities as discussion, discovery learning and open-ended questioning, usually related to their everyday experiences.
3 *Co-constructivist model*: where there is a dualist responsibility for learning which interconnects the roles of the learner and the teacher and thus emphasizes collaboration in the construction of knowledge.

The reception model dominated ideas about education for many centuries. For instance, during the Victorian era it was common to think of a child's mind as an 'empty vessel' to be filled up with knowledge 'poured in' by the teacher. This attitude to children continued to hold sway through much of the twentieth century and still has its supporters to this day. The constructivist model has its origins in the Romantic movement the late eighteenth and early nineteenth century and is fundamentally different from the reception model in that it views children as active seekers of knowledge who will learn best if provided opportunities to interact with the world around them. This method became most closely associated with the notion of 'child-centred' education which made its greatest impact on classrooms in the 1960s and 1970s but became increasingly discredited because it was seen as unstructured, impractical and difficult to manage. The co-constructivist model attempts to retain the best elements of each of the former models and has gained increasing support since the advent of the National Curriculum. It is this latter formulation on which this chapter focuses. The chapter goes on to argue that such an approach elides with recent developments at national level which attempt to integrate notions of creativity and personalization into the curriculum.

Co-construction and the curriculum

Those who take recent cognitive developmental theory seriously are increasingly dedicated to co-constructivist techniques (Broadfoot, 2000). This is because the twin perspectives of a 'top down' and 'bottom up' approach

(Biggs, 1992) spring both from pupils' experientially based attitudes and capabilities and the special features of subjects being taught which are perhaps clarified as challenges to pupils' stated positions. Dual transformations (framing curricular content within one's preconceptions in order to change one's preconceptions) align with the simple formulae devised by Adey and Shayer (1994) for teaching science to young adolescents, and Resnick *et al.* (1992) teaching mathematics to infants. The key issues of their concepts are as follows:

- Pupils' existing viewpoints are elicited, clarified and sanctioned as legitimate on topics to be discussed. Pupils realize what they already know.
- New knowledge challenges viewpoints already established. Pupils sense what they don't yet know and begin to probe for new meanings.
- Pupils seek to adapt the one set of viewpoints to the other through hypothetical and critical thinking, discussion, debate, argument, game-playing, trialling and so forth.
- Final syntheses are reached (if only provisionally), tasks accomplished and new tasks sighted.
- Pupils' viewpoints are elicited, clarified, etc., regarding the new tasks (Silcock and Brundrett, 2002).

The essence of partnership teaching (there are numerous formulations: see Hopkins and Reynolds, 2001; Silcock and Brundrett 2002; MacDonald, 2003) is that teachers acknowledge there are disparate pressures on their work and they bend consistently to pupil need (related to ability, aspiration, experience, commitment, etc.) while expecting pupils to reciprocate by accepting teacher monitoring and general guidance. In short, pupils and teachers work together to co-determine outcomes.

This bipartisan situation is not easily accomplished, given the likely conflicts of priority that arise in classrooms. That is why a key principle to establish with partnership work is the *distinctiveness* and yet equal validity of the different individual and social positions of pupils and teachers. As Dewey famously argued (1900; 1902; 1976), school curricula must engage directly with children's minds in schools if what is taught is to be enriching and meaningful for them. Curricula that do not respect the distinctiveness of pupil attitude can alienate rather than capture pupil interest because the pupils' views are not being taken into account and their favoured methods of learning are likely to be ignored. A first step towards reconciling teacher–pupil views is to recognize their differences while accepting that this may lead to the possibility of real conflict between teacher and pupil intention. Fortunately, such conflicts can actually lead to qualitative gains in learning (Johnson and Johnson, 1994) because they encourage staff and pupils to debate and discuss in order to come to agreements about one another's needs.

Partnership (or co-constructive) teaching has dual yet complementary aims, reflecting the legitimate yet distinct positions and needs of the partners while pointing to their interdependence. Namely, students develop personal perspectives on publicly valued knowledge and public perspectives on their personal lives, such that personal and public values enrich each other in a continuously evolving manner. There are three core principles that allow classroom strategies and evolving curricular interpretations to be decided pragmatically by teachers and pupils together:

1 A distinctiveness of teacher and pupil view generates twin-track or bipartisan school policies. All teaching decisions implicitly or explicitly respect worldviews built into publicly sanctioned curricula and informing learners' personal interests, attitudes, ambitions and so forth. That is, all main decisions and strategies respect the different viewpoints of pupils and teachers equally. *This is the partnership principle.*
2 Classroom practice roots itself in a resolving of conflicts of interest and opinion, informed by routine scepticism about what is taught. This scepticism arises naturally when pupil opinions are given equal worth to those of teachers. Put another way, school curricula are not treated as treasuries of received wisdom but as sets of propositions to be tested from the particular perspectives of pupils. Cognitive conflict is fertile soil for both public and personal improvement (sounding boards for each other). *This second principle is the need to accept, resolve and/or exploit conflicts of view.*
3 Partnership work should be regulated by democratic bargaining, even for those in close partnerships, so that, should one side have to act in the absence of the other, all decisions can in some sense be said to be democratically rule governed and so serve multiple ends. Partnership teaching nurtures democratic environments. *This is the democratic or contextual principle* (Silcock and Brundrett, 2002).

A main problem for partnership teaching is that pupils' inner worlds are privy only to pupils and one can never with certainty know exactly what pupils' need, expect or think in anything but a hit-and-miss way. But pupils themselves can 'scaffold' teachers' understanding of what is and is not useful for them to learn (in terms of their own perspectives), while teachers 'scaffold' pupils' thinking towards what is and is not publicly valued. Such dual tracking is hard in that it requires teachers to assess how well they are moving in two separate yet complementary directions. Yet it is exactly this judgement which informs teachers' planning and input. It helps them decide which curricular issues to explore and how these might be presented as propositions to be discussed or argued about (not provisional ideas masquerading as certainties).

Notably, the starting point for co-constructive teaching is for pupils to clarify what they already know. One can hardly adapt to other views if one is unclear about what one's own position is (it isn't just that teachers need to understand pupils' experiences; pupils need to understand their own experiences). Then it is the clarifying, challenging and restructuring which matter – i.e. curricular goals are in the main procedurally defined (process values) rather than reached through the teaching of a set content. Adey and Shayer (1994) think pupils must hypothesize and defend positions in the face of peer challenges and teacher questioning, not in a way so as to reveal some 'correct' view, but to lift learners to a hypothetico-deductive thinking typical of scientific debate. Resnick et al.'s (1992) intent is to overlap pupils conceiving of problems in their own intuitive language with those in a more formal mathematical language, not to show the first as wrong and the second as correct, but to force each to supervene on the other.

What teachers in this approach model is the reaching for an ever more challenging scepticism and questioning attitude. Because such a strategy is complex, it is worth elaborating on earlier discussion. The high-road climbing to a 'meta-cognitive' control over subjects (Adey and Shayer, 1994) comes through our subjecting ideas to challenges which, themselves, are evaluated as part of cross-perspective taking. Learners discover what challenges work, and which not, integrating these in the end within reliable, flexible, rule-governed operations. Metacognition (self-monitoring) is not just a form of hierarchical reflection or propensity for mental detachment. Piaget's ideal of formal-operations has meta-perspectives built into areas of knowledge, tools of any academic's trade. Recognizing that academic judgements are never more than staging points towards an ever subtler view is to keep a distance from known solutions, for ever having the option of reconceiving what is already known. The general process of cross-perspective taking implies seeing the way a single idea 'works' in diverse contexts – i.e. it must, as claimed above, prepare the ground for knowledge transfer.

Crucial to this sort of teaching is peer interaction whereby pupils habitually challenge, support, comment, evaluate and debate each other's standard views. A co-constructivist classroom is one where such talk is staple. Adey and Shayer's (1994; 1996) and Resnick et al.'s (1992; see also Kuhn, 1999) evidence is that such talk works not only with science teaching but also in developing critical states of mind (Piagetian formal operations; Vygotskian higher-order skills) and integrated forms of thinking (Broadfoot, 2000). Such ways of applying and testing out knowledge imply a 'no-holds barred' attitude which tolerates extensive disagreement. This attitude must be modelled by teachers themselves, who may well take a critical stance on public life, but by doing so acknowledge fashionable attitudes and contemporary idioms rather than ignore these.

This sort of teaching is unusual in the imaginative leaps required to blend radically opposing perspectives born from ability, gender, class, cultural background, personality and experience. It demands enough self-knowledge and knowledge of one's pupils to make the congruent integration of both a platform for conceptual change. This is after all what 'partnership' means: teaching and learning are cross-determined – notwithstanding the chance that learners, themselves, may not always consent to the contractual duties imposed. Over a period, and assuming any chance at all that learners become converted to educational values, this approach does have the merit of accepting the problem itself (the need to negotiate endemic conflicts) as real.

Self-restraint ought to be a byproduct of any sincere effort to work in a partnership manner – as should a flexible attitude towards curricular innovation. In pluralist settings, large groups will bring to task novel ambitions, insights, prejudices and so forth. To adapt to differences, synthesize arguments, defend in order to refine immature views, persist with a case until it can be over-ruled, and incite both dogged reasoning and flexibility of opinion is to be ubiquitous in a way not normally asked for within the intimate confines of classrooms. Democratic teaching may be shunned by some, because it faces up to social dilemmas we will otherwise avoid (Moore, 2000). It asks for the expression of disagreement and criticism, a probing for weaknesses and a search for person–group discord in order to reach a higher-order person–group accord.

Often, teachers will not find themselves teaching in the conventional sense, but mediating between options (Mason, 2000). They will put hypothetical alternatives to what is conventional in order to persuade learners to give up personal biases and standard beliefs for more promising ideas. So democratic teaching is not made easy by being cradled on a raft of social skills. One can imagine that the various capabilities listed will integrate differently according to that degree of conflict endemic in a school or classroom community: some inner-city schools demand a resoluteness of will not demanded in less stressful environments. Where pupils have an appetite for debate and criticism, a sound subject knowledge combined with a creative approach to problem-solving may well be a teacher's mainstay.

Notions of classroom management become in the end inseparable from notions of school management where all groups rightfully persuade individual members to swing into line behind rules to which they have, themselves, agreed. Generally speaking, this is not to be formulaic. There is no 'right' way to organize democratically.

A truly democratic education, which models society as a humane, egalitarian community, is one where the dominating context is the human one, with universal moral values as criteria for cross-cultural judgements. What democratic values create are contexts where individuals pursue self-chosen lifestyles without fear of oppression (providing they don't oppress others). A 'postmodern' culture without value priorities may only survive within a democratic state (as Kelly, 1995, argues), for it will be quite in order for postmodernists to establish their views as having parity with others. But it is hard to see how 'partnership' teaching can succeed where external pressures are non-democratic. A teacher impelled to deliver a curriculum without the consent of main stakeholders may well survive by deploying co-constructive, conflict resolution skills; but no one should underestimate the difficulties and hardships involved. The writers would like to suggest, however, that such co-construction of the curriculum is often the ideal way to ensure that creativity is embedded in pupil learning and it is to this topic that the chapter turns next.

ASK YOURSELF

- To what extent is the learning in your classroom and the classrooms of those in your team negotiated with the chidren, where appropriate?
- In what ways do teaching and learning opportunities facilitate and encourage debate?
- What opportunities are provided for the children to take ownership of their own learning within the parameters set by the teaching and other staff?

Creativity: not just an add-on

It has been suggested that 'creativity is a quality that most people prize, but which many of us struggle to prioritise' (Bentley, 2003: 1). This has certainly been the case in schools in recent years during a period where most institutions have struggled to integrate multiple initiatives and a dominant nationally imposed agenda for change which has included the National

Curriculum, national testing and inspection regimes and, more recently, national initiatives for literacy and numeracy. There has, however, been a resurgent interest in 'creativity' in primary schools in recent years which has been evidenced by the interest in the topic shown by national bodies in the field of education such as the QCA and the NCSL, who have reflected on a seminal report by the National Advisory Committee on Creative and Cultural Education (NACCCE) and attempted to produce guidance that will assist schools in integrating (or, depending on your perspective and length of experience, *reintegrating*) creative activity in the curriculum within the constraints of the National Curriculum.

All our Futures (NACCCE, 2000) defined 'creativity' as 'imaginative activity fashioned so as to produce outcomes that are both original and of value'; and 'creative education' was seen as 'forms of education that develop young people's capacities for original ideas and action' (NACCCE, 2000: 4). The report stated that we are all, or can be, creative to a greater or lesser extent and, most importantly, creativity is seen as 'a basic property of human intelligence' (page 4). *All our Futures* emphasized the extent to which creativity involves the exercise of imagination. *Leading the Creative School* (NCSL, 2002), which brought together 80 school leaders and policy-makers, was supported by the Innovation Unit, the DfES, DEMOS and QCA. This gathering revealed a growing interest in creativity in schools matched by a commitment from statutory organizations to explore the ways in which such creativity might be developed and enhanced. Key messages or suggestions that resulted from the event included the notions that school leaders should:

- 'start simply, build progressively' by having a manageable focus such as an event involving all staff and students that celebrates creative learning (page 4);
- 'build an environment for creative learning' through celebrating the pupil voice in displays in central areas of the school (page 4);
- 'find space for creativity' by allocating curriculum time for 'adventurous learning' (page 4);
- 'keep a clear focus on learning' by redesigning the way the curriculum is delivered to reflect learning needs (page 5);
- 'place a high premium on shared professional learning and development' by focusing professional development, building an expectation of creativity into the school's learning policy and working collaboratively (page 5); and
- build 'partnerships to sustain and enrich learning' (page 6).

Creativity should be valued for a number of other reasons (Bentley, 2003: 2). Creativity is, for instance, a major element in a successful economy and, as economic competition increases inexorably, there is pressure on organizations to create new products and services in order to 'achieve continuous improvement and renewal' (Bentley, 2003: 2). Moreover, in a more open society where social identities are less fixed by tradition, there are new opportunities for people to shape their won identities in a 'choice-driven world' (2003: 2). This mixture of economic necessity and values-driven change provides a powerful incentive to enhance creative activity at all levels in society.

Indeed, we must remember that creativity is a highly contested concept and is subject to a variety of definitions that have interesting inter-relationship with differing perspectives in psychological theory, attitudes to cognition and beliefs about the ends associated with education. This reinvigoration of interest in creativity has implications for our attitudes to learning and teaching. Bentley has argued that 'creative learners are people who understand the potential to learn from any and all of their encounters with the world' (2003: 2) and 'also relates to the ability of learners, both as individuals and groups, to develop strategies for self-directed learning, and for reflecting and recognising different kinds of value in learning experience' (2003: 2). The four key qualities associated with this perspective are seen as 'the ability to formulate new problems'; 'the ability to transfer what one learns across different contexts'; 'the ability to recognise that learning is an ongoing, incremental process'; and 'the capacity to focus one's attention in pursuit of a goal' (2003: 3).

The QCA also built on the work of the NACCCE and the document *Creativity: Find It, Promote It* (QCA, 2004) shows a commendably overt and broad commitment to developing the creative life of schools. The QCA debate the three characteristics of the NACCCE report which are defined as 'imagination and purpose', 'originality' and 'value' (QCA, 2004: 1–2) and they go on to suggest that teachers can promote pupils' creativity by:

- planning tasks and activities that give pupils opportunities to be creative; and
- teaching in a way that makes the most of pupils' creativity.

Such exhortation may seem obvious but they emphasize the need for both planning and pedagogy to ensure that creativity is embedded in the curriculum and individual learning opportunities. Moreover, the QCA guidance on leading for creativity goes on to offer much greater specificity and detail and provides a helpful analysis of the roles of staff at different levels in the leadership and management structure, including middle leaders. This guidance is summarized below:

Promoting creativity when planning

- Set a clear purpose for pupils' work.
- Be clear about freedoms and constraints.
- Fire pupils' imagination through other learning and experiences.
- Give pupils opportunities to work together.

Promoting creativity when teaching

- Establish criteria for success.
- Capitalize on unexpected learning opportunities.
- Ask open-ended questions and encourage critical reflection.
- Regularly review work in progress.

How can teams of teachers promote creativity?

- Ask yourself how you could work together to improve pupils' ability to ask questions; to explore ideas and alternatives; and to evaluate ideas and actions.
- What aspects of pupils' creative thinking and behaviour might best be promoted through your particular subject?
- Ask each teacher in your team to identify an opportunity for promoting pupils' creativity in a planned lesson or activity and to build a creativity objective into the subject-specific objectives (for example, to promote pupils' ability to ask questions or explore ideas).
- As a team, talk about how you could achieve these creativity objectives.
- After the lessons, come back together as a team and compare and discuss outcomes.

How can senior managers and governors promote creativity?

- Value creativity as a school.
- Encourage professional learning and development.
- Build partnerships to enrich learning.
- Provide opportunities for pupils to work with creative people.
- Provide a stimulating physical environment.
- Manage time effectively.
- Celebrate pupils' creativity (QCA, 2004).

These issues denote a commitment to intrinsic motivation and a commitment to challenging current practice and 'chance taking' in pedagogical activity which articulate with the central contention of this chapter – that pupils and teachers need to work together in defining and developing the curriculum within the legitimate constrains of the national agenda.

Case study: St Mary's Primary

St Mary's is a Roman Catholic primary school situated in a thriving market town in the north Midlands/north west of England. The school is structured into seven classes and has 180 children on role. There are seven teachers and four teaching assistants employed at the school. The school applied for the 'Arts Mark', awarded by the Arts Council of England, in 2001. The process of application was complex and lengthy and it took three months to complete the application process. St Mary's was successful in its application and held the award for three years, at which point it became eligible to reapply for Arts Mark status. At this stage the school is the only one in the area to hold such an award and is, therefore, the focus of some interest in the educational community.

The environment of St Mary's bears testament to the creative abilities of staff and pupils since there are very high-quality displays of art, craft, writing and other curriculum subjects displayed on the walls of the school. The school holds an 'Arts Week' which has been running annually for three years. Themes have included an African Arts week during which time everything to do with literacy and numeracy was related to this topic. 'It's like a week's party', the arts co-ordinator stated. An Arts Club has been in operation for four years and there are two drama clubs: one for Key Stage 1 and one for Key Stage 2.

The headteacher of St Mary's views curriculum development and creative activity as being 'very collective'. He sees his main role as encouraging and enabling: 'I know how to facilitate it', as he put it. The headteacher's capacity, and willingness, to delegate was attested to by the arts co-ordinator.

Much of the responsibility for developing creative activity inevitably falls on an individual who is at middle leadership level in the school. As the head stated: 'Invariably there is a person who brings the things together.' The school is, therefore, fortunate to have a talented and well trained arts co-ordinator who is also responsible for special needs education and who sees an interesting inter-relationship between the two areas of work in the school.

The QCA guidelines (2004) were welcomed by the school, mainly because they provided an affirmation of interest in the topic: 'It's good to see that creativity is more recognized because there was a time when things like arts and sport were not recognized but we draw on a wide range of materials' (arts co-ordinator). The QCA materials had not, however, had a very great impact on the school and its work. QCA overall guidance was, though, one of the key factors in planning for creative activity. The school had used the local authority scheme but found that the general QCA National Curriculum materials conformed to the structure that staff have become used to and so the QCA materials remain at the centre of planning. Equally it was clear that the 'Internet is a big resource' (arts co-ordinator).

The commitment to children with differing sets of intellectual skills was also reaffirmed within this overall sense of mission: 'Part of our mission is to develop people with diverse gifts' (head).

Thus it seems that creative activity is promoted in a number of ways at St Mary's. The commitment of the head and staff is important and the role of the curriculum co-ordinator was central. Creative activity is developed within the overall guidelines set out in the National Curriculum but occasions are sought out when 'space', both physical and temporal, is made available to staff, parents and children, to undertake wide-ranging creative experiences that may offer key moments in a child's development.

Every Child Matters and personalized learning: a new agenda for the curriculum

Every Child Matters (DfES, 2003), the government's vision for children's services, proposed reshaping children's services to help achieve a number of key outcomes which included the aims that children should:

- be healthy;
- stay safe;
- enjoy and achieve;
- make a positive contribution; and
- achieve economic well-being.

Despite this impressive list of aspirations, the thinking behind *Every Child Matters* is not new for most, if not all, schools. As the DfES acknowledge: 'A combination of high expectations, innovative thinking and a broad view of supporting children and young people are common features of highly successful schools' (2003: 3). The aspiration is that strong, autonomous schools will be well placed to collaborate with directors of children's services and local authorities as they develop children's trust arrangements and children and young people's plans. To this end it is expected that school staff will develop good relationships with other practitioners such as social workers, nurses, GPs and educational psychologists. As part of this agenda the notion of personalized learning has come to the fore and, as was also the case in the previous section about creativity, its core ideas are increasingly embedded in the work of central organizations whose work impacts on learning and teaching such as the NCSL, the TTA, the QCA and Ofsted. The Teaching and Learning Research Programme (TLRP), one of the largest educational research initiatives ever mounted, has undertaken a series of major research studies on the topic of personalized learning. The report of the TLRP group notes that in September 2004 the DfES produced a new version of the five key components of personalized learning. They were as follows:

1 Assessment for learning and the use of evidence and dialogue to identify every pupil's learning needs.
2 Teaching and learning strategies that develop the competence and confidence of every learner by actively engaging and stretching them.
3 Curriculum entitlement and choice that delivers breadth of study, personal relevance and flexible learning pathways through the system.
4 A student-centred approach to school organization, with school leaders and teachers thinking creatively about how to support high-quality teaching and learning.
5 Strong partnership beyond the school to drive forward progress in the classroom, to remove barriers to learning and to support pupil well-being. (Pollard and James, 2004: 3).

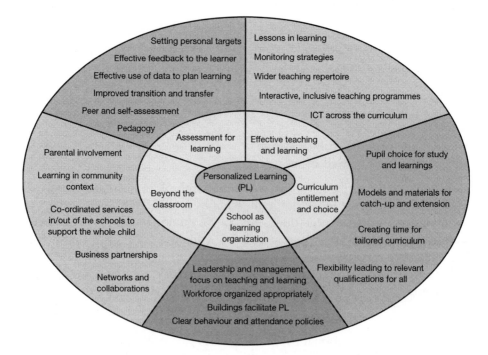

Figure 11.1 Key components of personalized learning
Source: Pollard and James (2004: 4)
Crown copyright material is reproduced with the permission of the Controller of HMSO and the Queen's Printer for Scotland

The TLRP report uses the key components to construct the model of personalized learning outlined in Figure 11.1. The model reveals that personalized learning consists of five core elements supplemented by an enormous but loosely defined range of policies and practices, including the following:

- Giving pupils opportunities to decide their own learning objectives.
- Providing guidance on asking questions, giving feedback and using criteria.
- Helping pupils assess their own and one another's learning.
- Giving pupils opportunities to assess one another's work (Pollard and James, 2004: 6).

The report goes on to acknowledge the importance of group work but accepts that such activities can be resisted by teachers, especially when preparing children for external testing (Pollard and James, 2004: 8). To overcome such fears case studies are offered which seem to indicate that certain key actions can improve practice in relation to group activities. These include the following:

- Build support among staff (who may be sceptical) by presenting evidence of the positive outcomes of consultation, drawing on the work of a small group of teachers and pupils in your own school or reported work from other schools.
- Be sensitive to the anxiety experienced by teachers who have not before consulted pupils about teaching and learning – and also pupils' concerns and anxieties.
- Ensure that other school policies and initiatives are in harmony with the principles and values that underpin pupil consultation and that all areas of school life offer opportunities for pupils' voices to be heard (Pollard and James, 2004: 13).

It has to be acknowledged that a number of dangers exist in relation to the agenda on personalized learning since the policy challenges the mutual accommodations which often grow up in routine teacher–pupil classroom practices and calls for high expectations, positive responses and new forms of learner-aware pedagogy. Thus it is vital that this new and important agenda is followeded through, on the ground, with appropriate support and accountability systems (Pollard and James, 2004: 25). Nonetheless, personalized learning holds out a number of possibilities, including: a more partnership-oriented relationship between pupils and teachers; a basis for developing democratic principles and practices; and a more inclusive approach to school self-evaluation. Such policies fit squarely with the co-constructionist approaches advocated in this chapter.

Summary

Co-constructed systems of leadership hold out the possibility of empowering all the stakeholders in the school, including pupils and parents, as part of the decision-making process. Under such a system, at the same time, the legitimate authority of the leader, whether he or she is at senior or middle management level, will be safeguarded. As we seek to inculcate and enhance values in teaching and learning it is important to develop this values dimension in leadership.

The late 1990s and early twenty-first century have seen a movement away from the more reductivist aspects of the rigid National Curriculum and schools are being encouraged, once again, to develop practices that will encourage creativity in learning and teaching and engage with individual pupils. All this is to be applauded but such initiatives present some striking challenges to teachers who remain under increasing pressure to ensure the highest outcomes in external assessment. Some teachers, especially those whose experiences span the period back to the heady days of the child-centred curriculum in the 1960s and 1970s, may say that there is nothing new here and that we are merely reintegrating practices that were lost with the advent of the National Curriculum. There is much truth in this but the main challenge of the coming years is to develop creative practice and to engage with individual learners as part of ensuring enhanced outcomes, in the broadest sense. One of the great gains of the post-National Curriculum era has been a huge development on the metalanguage of pedagogy at classroom and school level. An equal sophistication is now needed as schools try to balance rigour, creativity and personalization in the curriculum. Inevitably experienced middle leaders in primary schools will be at the centre of these initiatives since they are in a unique position to provide a link between classroom practice and senior leadership in schools.

References

Adey, P. and Shayer, M. (1994) *Really Raising Standards*. London: Routledge.

Adey, P. and Shayer, M. (1996) 'An exploration of long-term transfer effects following an extended intervention program in the high school science curriculum', in L. Smith (ed.) *Critical Readings in Paiget*. London: Routledge.

Bentley, T. (2003) *Distributed Intelligence: Leadership and Learning*. Nottingham: National College for School Leadership.

Biggs, J.B. (1992) 'Returning to school: review and discussion', in A. Dimetriou et al. (eds) Neo-Paigetian Theories of Cognitive Development: Implications and Applications for Education. London: Routledge.

Broadfoot, P. (2000) 'Liberating the learner through assessment', in J. Collins and D. Cook (eds) Understanding Learning: Influences and Outcomes. London: Paul Chapman Publishing/Open University Press.

Carnell, E. and Lodge, C. (2005) 'Leading for effective learning', in M. Coleman and P. Earley (eds) Leadership and Management in Education: Cultures, Change and Context. Oxford: Oxford University Press.

Dewey, J. (1900) The Child and Society. Chicago, IL: University of Chicago Press.

Dewey, J. (1902) The Child and the Curriculum. Chicago, IL: University of Chicago Press.

Dewey, J. (1976) The School and Society. Carbondale, IL: Arcturus Books (a facsimile of the first edition published in 1899).

DfES (2003) Every Child Matters: Change for Children in Schools. London: DfES.

Gardner, H. (1993) The Unschooled Mind. London: Fontana.

Goleman, D. (1996) Emotional Intelligence. London: Bloomsbury.

Hopkins, D. and Reynolds, D. (2001) 'The past, present and future of school improvement: towards the Third Age', British Educational Research Journal, 27: 459–75.

Johnson, D.W. and Johnson, R.T. (1994) 'Constructive conflict in the schools', Journal of Social Issues, 50: 117–37.

Kelly, A.V. (1995) Education and Democracy, Principles and Practices. London: Paul Chapman Publishing.

Kuhn, D. (1999) 'A developmental model of critical thinking', Educational Researcher, 28: 16–26.

MacDonald, D. (2003) 'Curriculum change and the post-modern world: is the school curriculum-reform movement an anachromism?', Journal of Curriculum Studies, 35: 139–49.

Marton, F., Dall'Allba, G. and Beaty, E. (1993) 'Conceptions of learning', International Journal of Educational Research, 19: 277–300.

Mason, M. (2000) Teachers as critical mediators of knowledge, Journal of Philosophy of Education, 34, 2: 343–52.

Middlewood, D. and Burton, N. (eds) (2001) Managing the Curriculum. London: Paul Chapman Publishing.

Moore, R. (2000) For knowledge, tradition, progressivism and progress in Education: reconstructing the curriculum debate, Cambridge Journal of Education, 31, 1: 17–36.

NACCCE (2000) *Creativity and Cultural Education: All Our Futures: A Summary*. London: National Campaign for the Arts.

NCSL (2002) *Leading the Creative School: A Leading Edge Seminar*. Nottingham: NCSL.

Pollard, A. and James, M. (2004) *Personalised Learning: A Commentary by the Teaching and Learning Research Programme*. London: TLRP/ESRC.

QCA (2004) *Creativity: Find It, Promote It*. London: QCA.

Resnick, L.B., Bill, V. and Lesgold, S. (1992) 'Developing thinking abilites in arithmetic class,' in A. Dimetriou *et al.* (eds) *Neo-Paigetian Theories of Cognitive Development: Implications and Applications for Education*. London: Routledge.

Richmond, K. (1971) *The School Curriculum*. London: Methuen.

Silcock, P. and Brundrett, M. (2002) *Competence, Success and Excellence in Teaching*. London: RoutledgeFalmer.

Recommended reading

Fox, R. (2005) *Teaching and Learning: Lessons from Psychology*. Oxford: Blackwell.

Middlewood, D. and Burton, N. (eds) (2001) *Managing the Curriculum*. London: Paul Chapman Publishing.

Websites

Pollard, A. and James, M. (2004) *Personalised Learning: A Commentary by the Teaching and Learning Research Programme* (http://www.standards.dfes.gov.uk/personalisedlearning/downloads/tlrppamphlet.pdf).

QCA (2004) *Creativity: Find It, Promote It* (www.ncaction.org.uk/creativity/promote.htm).

QCA (2005) *How can you Promote Creativity?* (http://www.ncaction.org.uk/creativity/promote.htm).

12

Classroom and school-based research for evidence-based decision-making

LEARNING OUTCOMES OF THIS CHAPTER

By the end of this chapter you should be able to:

- understand the importance of evidence-based decision-making
- recognize the purposes and the context of research
- articulate and analyse key concepts such as populations, samples, constraints, tools and strategies
- analyse data and present recommendations to staff

Evidence-based decision-making

In the classroom teachers are continually required to analyse feedback from their classes and respond by making decisions on the best course of action to follow. While at the end of sessions it is possible to reflect and evaluate the various performances and the decisions made, during taught sessions the teacher much show great awareness of the dynamics of the classroom and make timely and appropriate interventions to effect a positive development of learning. To make this possible teachers need to develop a bank of strategies based upon best practice obtained from a variety of sources and honed by experience. When, on reflection, teachers decide that a more fundamental change in their practice or approach is required, rather than looking within themselves, they need to explore ideas beyond their immediate experience to gain a wider, refreshed perspective on the issues. If current strategies or approaches to teaching are not as effective as desired, then it is necessary to consider doing something different. By carrying out research, reviewing recently published findings and theories, it is possible to arrive at potential 'something different's' to try. In this sense research in schools exists to underpin the commitment to change and school improvement, explored in Chapter 5, and there is a close relationship between the notion of research and the concepts encapsulated in the techniques of evaluation, outlined in Chapter 6.

This chapter explores the value of research as a means of systematically inquiring to provide a foundation for school improvement and the gathering of evidence to establish how effective the 'improvement' has been, and traces the relationship between research and evaluation. In particular it examines the different forms of research available to school-based practitioners and suggests ways in which research can be structured and reported upon to inform the strategic decision-making within schools. School-based research is claimed by Joyce (1991) to be one of the five 'doors' to improve practice within schools. Subject leaders, through an investigation of their own practice as teachers and leaders, will be able to gather the evidence on which to base decisions affecting innovation and change within the school. Through direct involvement with the basis of the decision-making processes they will be able to take ownership of the issues and make the options available more meaningful. In this way we wish to show that systematic inquiry into specific elements of teaching is a hard but crucial component of continuing professional development – and a key to raising the esteem in which the profession is held. This accords with the DfEE strategy for continuing professional development which states: 'We want to encourage teachers, as reflective practitioners, to think about what they do well, to reflect on what they could share with colleagues, as well as identifying their own learning needs' (2001: 12). In our view teachers need to be seen as equal partners with academic researchers in the process of producing evidence about teaching and in using it to raise standards.

The purposes of research

Morrison (2002: 3) suggests that educational research has a twin focus:

1 *Attitudinal*: 'a distinctive way of thinking about educational phenomena'.
2 *Action*: a systematic means of investigating them.

Brown and Dowling (1998: 165) make an attempt to distinguish between 'professional educational practice' – the reflective practitioner – and 'educational research practice', which tries to address and understand the deeper issues underlying educational phenomena, asking the question 'why?' not just the more immediate and more practical considerations of 'what?' and 'how?' This suggests that, while educational research will certainly influence what happens in the classroom, the major force of its impact will be on the long-term policy decisions made within the school.

As far as schools are concerned, one of the major benefits of educational research is the dissemination of the identification, clarification and generalization of perceptions of good and effective practice. This allows schools to benefit from the improvements in practice elsewhere, using the findings as a starting point for developing their own practice. The dissemination of research findings and the investigation of effective practice, in all aspects of school life, were one of the founding principles of the National College for School Leadership (NCSL, 2004), which acts as a sponsor and clearing house of educational research for school improvement.

Some researchers, such as Burgess (Bryman and Burgess, 1994) and Hammersley (1995), take the view that educational research should take the form of a 'disinterested inquiry'. While it is undoubtedly essential to maintain a sense of objectivity and even perspective, the key rationale for research, as it is performed by practitioners in school, is ultimately to lead to an improvement in the educational provision. A major motivator for researchers in schools is that they *are* interested!

An exploration of the nature of educational research leads to an inevitable focus on perceptions of reality and the way we construct theories to explain those realities. Everybody has a unique perception of reality which biases the collection, interrogation and analysis of evidence. However, similarities in perceptions make it possible to group together those holding a similar set of beliefs. These may be implicit or explicit but they do express a view about what is 'normal' and provide a coherent 'worldview' or paradigm. If this is not acknowledged it may appear as though the research is carrying a 'hidden agenda' for a particular cause or source of bias. 'Constructivism' and 'feminism' are examples of paradigms presenting a particular perspective on learning and social structure which will impact on the approach to and findings from a research activity.

To oversimplify the situation enormously for the sake of brevity (a much more comprehensive discussion of these issues can be found in specialist educational research texts such as Cohen *et al.*, 2000, and Coleman and Briggs, 2002), educational research can be reduced to two main approaches: positivism and interpretivism. Essentially, positivism attempts to apply theory(ies) to the research context to assess how applicable they are – to compare an (often idealized) model of reality (the theory) with reality. An example of this might be research to discover how successfully a school is accommodating different learning styles in its lesson planning. This implies that research should focus on the observable and the measurable – whether in absolute terms (sampling lesson plans for VAK (visual, audio, kinaesthetic) inputs, for example) or via perceptions of relevant individuals or groups of individuals (how confident do teachers feel putting VAK plans into effect?). This relationship with the evidence base tends to link positivism with quantitative research where the measurement of variables and concept formation has a central role and the focus of the research is concerned with the nature of causality. Interpretivism is a more 'people-centred' approach which acknowledges the integration of the research within the research environment, where each impact on the perceptions and understandings of the other. Interpretivists will immerse themselves in the research environment and attempt to 'explore the "meanings" of events and phenomena from the subjects' perspectives' (Morrison, 2002: 18) (e.g. observing group dynamics when pupils are provided with different stimuli and equipment for mathematics sessions). The evidence collected by interpretivists will be qualitative in nature, offering a rich and deep description of the research environment as a unique context. While positivism will impose a direction and focus on the research, interpretivism will be driven by the subject, thus adopting a much more holistic, longitudinal perspective. Comparability is not a particular concern to interpretivists as the research becomes the unique 'story teller' where the story had no discernible or definitive conclusion; but for the positivist, comparability is all important.

Clearly the two different approaches are both applicable to the work of a subject leader, and the purposes to which the outcomes of the research is to be put will be the main determinant. If the focus of the research is to attempt to apply or assess the 'readiness' of a particular approach to learning, teaching or planning that appears to be successful elsewhere, then, clearly, a positivist approach would be the obvious choice. If the focus is more concerned with 'why do less able pupils appear not to enjoy maths activities?', then there is the potential for an interpretivist approach to be taken. Generally, though, where the focus of the research effort is on school improvement, then it is likely that a positivist approach will be adopted, leaving the interpretivist approach to 'hardcore' researchers.

While full-time academics and researchers in the field of education would argue that educational research should aim to increase our knowledge and understanding of educational phenomena, in the context of this book we should perhaps temper our aims to focus on improving our knowledge of the education within the school with the aim of improving the quality of learning and teaching by providing evidence to influence the decision-making processes. By restricting the parameters the task can be made more manageable for the teacher-researcher.

- How often do I read about the outcomes of classroom-based research?
- Have I made use of reports of research to improve my own practice?
- What forms of research do I find most convincing – quantitative or qualitative?
- Do I perceive the realities of my school differently from other staff?

Effective and convincing research emerges as a result of careful planning and consistency of focus. It is based upon a clear appreciation of the issues arising out of a thorough analysis of the context, which is then used to formulate a set of questions to focus the research effort. Previous research in the area and relevant theories are analysed to offer potential 'ways forward'. A knowledge of research methods is necessary in order to chose the most effective means of gathering the necessary evidence, which is then analysed in respect of the theories and past research. Only then is it possible to use the evidence to justify a particular course of action that can be recommended to the school. The following sections take you through this process in more detail.

Locating the context of the research

Before going in search of answers, it is essential to identify and clarify the questions and confirm that the *right* questions are being asked. There are several stages to work through here, the first being to clarify the context to reveal the key issues that need to be addressed. This context may be driven by external factors (such as a government initiative to encourage schools to plan cross-curricularly) or school-focused issues (perceived lack of staff subject knowledge); in either case the perception of importance needs to be confirmed – is it just your worry or is the matter of wider concern within the school? Effectively you need to do some preliminary, anecdotal research in order to confirm the importance of the issues and to clarify possible links with other issues the school is attempting to address. Analyse the context to identify those factors which are considered to have a significant influence on the situation. What is known about these factors already? This could mean referring to existing policy documents or the findings of the most recent Ofsted report to establishing the starting point for finding out more.

From this analysis it should be possible to identify a small number of key questions that you need to address, and hopefully answer, through your research – you will need to refer back to these questions to maintain the focus during the course of the research activity. The final aspect of locating the research is the identification of the field of knowledge that should provide a conceptual framework on which to construct the research tools which will be used to gather the evidence.

ASK YOURSELF

- ◆ Currently, what are the most pressing issues for my subject in my school?
- ◆ Why are these issues important, and are they important to anybody else?
- ◆ What could I find out about them?
- ◆ What do I need to find out about them?

Exploring the existing body of knowledge

Even when the field of knowledge that you need to examine has been identified, performing a review of that information can be a quite daunting task. Given that over 33,000 academic books and 400 educational journals are published in the UK each year, the chance of finding the piece of information that you need to innovate your school's needs would appear to be quite remote – and this is without taking into account all the English language publications from other countries.

Searching for information can be a very time-consuming task, even with good search skills. While Internet search engines and electronic education library catalogues, once primed with the most appropriate key terms, might just provide a list of promising titles to browse through there are still problems to address. In the case of the web, it is the reliability of the sources that must be closely questioned. Specific site searches, such as those of UK government bodies (Ofsted, DfES, TTA, Teachernet), educational organizations (NCSL, QCA, and subject associations such as ASE) and universities (.ac.uk or .edu in the USA), may be more fruitful in the long run than general searches, unless the search is restricted to more reliable sources. In the case of books, there is still the need to go into the library (if access is permitted) and actually browse through the books to see if the content is finally relevant.

Possibly the best source, at least in the first instance, may well be colleagues who already have a knowledge of the field. These are likely to be specialists such as advisory teachers, education tutors, subject association field officers, more experienced subject leaders in other schools or Beacon Schools (2004), which specialize in that particular aspect of education. If they are unable to provide the information directly there is a strong possibility that they will be able to recommend appropriate sources in order to narrow the search.

Where recommended sources are dated further searches can be performed using author details or, in the case of journals, by browsing through the most recent issues. More general issues will often be reported upon by the educational press and an online search of back issues can open up new lines of inquiry. Once you have identified your source make a careful note of it so that you can find it again should you need to. For electronic sources it is worth while downloading the relevant pages while you have them on screen rather than relying on the availability on the server at the current address at a later date.

The literature that you have sourced should be compared and contrasted to reveal the strengths and weaknesses inherent in different approaches to the issues that you have identified. Based upon your insights and knowledge of the school context, it would be possible to build up an understanding of what approaches are likely to meet with success and so construct a bespoke model derived from the different sources accessed. Or it could be a matter of identifying a couple of different approaches that are likely to achieve the outcomes that you want, and these can either be put to staff for a decision by discussion or piloted so that the relative success can be compared.

ASK YOURSELF

- ◆ Do I have a subject mentor or colleague whom I can turn to for sources or advice?
- ◆ Can I gain access to appropriate sources of information?
- ◆ Do I have the necessary skills to search for information?

The following three sections focus on three key questions which will determine the nature of the research and evidence collection:

1 What are you going to ask?
2 Whom are you going to ask?
3 How are you going to ask?

Developing research tools from your reading

This is where you clarify, with the help of your reading and other external input, precisely what it is you want to find out from the research – the key questions that you want the evidence to reveal answers to. It is possible that the same research task has been performed elsewhere and that the same tools (questionnaires, observation sheets, pupil assessments, etc.) can be used with minor alterations to take account of contextual differences. For example, teaching observation sheets provided for use with trainee teachers might be adapted for use with experienced teachers working within a specific subject context. Rather than adapting a single tool, it is more likely that there will be an amalgam of several different questionnaires or observation sheets (etc.) and then changes made for context.

Where there are no existing tools, the theory should be used as the basis for the development of one. Essentially this will mean examining the theory in detail to produce a list of questions or key points, which, when taken together, will provide the evidence that you require to answer the overarching research questions that you have set.

While you may well have a particular research methodology in mind during the development of the tool, the actual approach that you adopt may be constrained, forcing you to adapt an existing tool so that it can be applied in a different way. How can you use an existing research tool which is in the format of a classroom observation sheet when you cannot be released from your own class to observe? For this reason it can be quite useful to deconstruct existing tools to their basic components so that they can be reconstructed to take account of context and methodology. For example, an existing observation schedule designed to capture the quality and focus of pupil–pupil and pupil–teacher verbal interactions in science sessions may be reconstructed into a simple questionnaire that pupils and their teacher can be asked to complete – in addition to querying the number of interactions (questions, instructions, etc.), it would also be possible to ask pupils their perceptions about the quality and usefulness of those interactions (something that the observation would not have directly revealed).

It is essential to link the construction of the tool back to the theory in order to make the final analysis of the evidence (your findings) against expectations (the theory) as smooth as possible. It also confirms the importance of finding out more about the issues through reading and exploring other existing sources of information prior to constructing the final research tools.

- ◆ What does the theory suggest I should be asking?
- ◆ Are there any existing tools that I could adapt for my purposes?
- ◆ Will the research tool give me the evidence that I need to answer my questions?

Populations, samples and constraints

To a large extent the question of 'whom are you going to ask?' (who will be the research population) will have already have been answered when you analysed the context and identified the important factors (including people and groups of people) when the parameters of the research were being formulated. However, knowing whom you want to ask and getting access to them can be very different propositions. Also, do you ask everybody within that particular group or just a selection? And, if so, how do you select? Much of this depends on the nature of the research activity. If, for example, the focus of the research is to assess the use of art equipment and materials throughout the school, then all classes will need to participate. If, on the other hand, the focus is on the use of particular teaching strategies to improve the quality of still-life drawing, then it may, in the first instance, be more appropriate to focus on a small number of classes with like-minded teachers who are more likely to be successful, prior to rolling out the approach across the school.

Where parents are a key respondent group (a research focus on arrangements for educational visits, for instance), then sampling may become more of an issue – as a consequence of expense (the production of questionnaires) or time (your time in collating the responses for questionnaires or carrying out interviews). Ideally, the sampling of the population will reduce the number of respondents to more manageable levels without appreciably reducing the quality or range of the responses. Essentially there are two general approaches to sampling – probability and non-probability. Probability approaches assume a degree of randomness – if a 10 per cent sample of the parents of 200 pupils is deemed to be an appropriate sample size for a questionnaire then the questionnaires could be given out to:

- 20 pupils at random;
- every tenth pupil on the register alphabetically (systematically);
- five pupils in each year group in Key Stage 2 (stratified sample); or
- 20 pupils in a class chosen randomly (cluster sample).

to take home to their parent(s). Non-probability methods of sampling include convenience sampling (giving a questionnaire to the first 20 parents to collect their children from school one evening); judgemental sampling (the first 20 parents to attend a parents' evening); and quota sampling (choosing by ethnic group or pupil ability). Whichever approach is taken to sample the population it should be chosen in a rational way to give confidence in the validity of the findings (further details of sampling techniques can be found in Cohen *et al.*, 2000, and Fogelman in Coleman and Briggs, 2002).

While 'case study' is usually taken to be a research methodology, it more closely resembles an approach to sampling. By focusing on a particular case to study, be it a school, class, teacher or pupil, it is the concentration on a specific example taken from a (usually much larger) population. Once the case study is chosen, usually on the basis of convenience (your school or class), then a number of research strategies can still be brought to bear.

Research strategies: survey, observation, documentary analysis, action research

In choosing how best to ask the questions there will be a compromise between the methodologies that will provide the most valid, full and accurate responses and those that are possible given the constraints of time, resources and effort. It is pointless choosing a route which requires a research team of 20 and £100,000 if you are on your own and the head wants you to report back by the end of term! 'What do I want to do?' needs to be tempered with 'what can I do?' – there is no disgrace remarking that further research is required when you complete your study (at least you have evidence to show that outcome!).

When deciding upon an approach the aim must be to obtain a valid, reliable evidence base in a format which can be analysed in a meaningful and coherent way. While a survey, in the form of a questionnaire, is often seen as the 'easy option' the questions and logistics to distribute and retrieve the papers need to be very carefully considered. Pilot studies are usually recommended to iron our difficulties with the questionnaire – are the instructions clear? Does it provide responses in the format expected? Does it take 'too long' to complete? Are any issues left unresolved? Response rates may vary significantly depending on the nature of the respondents – a class of pupils can be asked to complete a questionnaire there and then for a 100 per cent return, but one sent to parents to explore the reasons for non-attendance at parent–teacher consultations may well have a less successful response rate.

One of the key reasons for using questionnaires is the potential for anonymity but it is helpful to have some background information from the respondent to help interpret and locate their responses. For teachers, particularly where an outcome from the research might be the provision of additional training, it would be helpful to know how long they have worked at the school, how long they have been in teaching, etc. – from this it might be possible to determine whether the lack of confidence in pupils using calculators in the classroom was randomly spread throughout the school or just an issue for teachers who had only quite recently been employed.

At the heart of a good questionnaire is a series of precise, unambiguous and well focused questions structured so that the respondent can answer them quickly and easily. Time needs to be taken by the author of the questionnaire to make life easy for the respondent. A question quoted by Bell (in Coleman and Briggs, 2002) highlights many of these problems: 'Is the quality of the teaching, support and supervision in college and on placements good?' (2002: 163). Apart from being a confusing multi-part question it asks the respondent to do too much in the form of a meaningful response – even assuming that terms such as 'support' and 'supervision' have clear meaning. It is difficult to understand how the researcher would have been able to collate the wide range of responses that would have been likely from such a question. A reworking, using the same terminology, could resolve the situation for both researcher and respondent: 'Please rate the quality of the *teaching*, *support* and *supervision* in *college* and on *placements* on a scale of 1(excellent) to 5 (poor) in each of the cells below' (see Figure 12.1).

	Teaching	Support	Supervision
College			
Placement			

Figure 12.1 Reworked questionnaire

Clearly, there is the potential for respondents to place different relative values on ratings of 2, 3 and 4, but all that can be asked for are perceptions, not absolute values. Respondents can be asked to rate their level of agreement with statements, as shown in Figure 12.2.

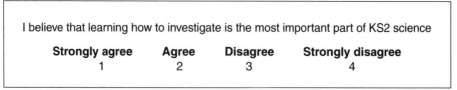

I believe that learning how to investigate is the most important part of KS2 science

Strongly agree   **Agree**   **Disagree**   **Strongly disagree**
1   2   3   4

Figure 12.2 Ratings on a Likert scale

This Likert scale is a four-point scale, but they can be any number from 3 to 7. An even number of options is usually employed to avoid neutral responses.

It is often worth while placing a couple of more 'open' questions at the end of the questionnaire to allow the respondent to elaborate on previous answers or offer further comment on the issues under discussion. Always thank the respondent and clearly explain the procedures for returning the completed questionnaire (where to and by when).

Interviews need to be at least as carefully planned as questionnaires with a schedule of questions or focus points – which need to be unambiguous, unbiased and clear. They are superior to questionnaires in that they allow for a feedback loop to enable the interviewer to respond to the answers given and delve more deeply into particular issues as they arise. Since interviews are relatively time-consuming, it is important that the right individuals are chosen and the most effective techniques are applied. A series of closed questions can be completed using a questionnaire – usually quicker and easier for both parties, so the focus should be to explore specific issues in depth, perhaps to supplement information obtained via other sources.

While interviews clearly lack the anonymity of questionnaires, they must still remain confidential. Even so, the relationship between the interviewer and the interviewee will have a potentially critical impact on the validity and reliability of the responses – the question 'how do you rate the support for English given by the head in this school?' might well get different responses from the same interviewee if the interviewer were the English subject leader rather than the headteacher. As interviews will tend to be face to face (rather than via telephone, for example) the response will not just be the words themselves but how they are said and the body language that accompanies them. Before the interview starts, there must be agreement on how it is to be recorded and reported – taping or videoing takes a great deal of time to transcribe, but this must be weighed against the possibility of responses being misreported or missed entirely with written notes. It might be useful to send a copy of the completed notes to the interviewee to check for accuracy and meaning.

For it to be meaningful, observation needs to be structured and focused and, ethically, needs to be agreed by both parties, although there are very important debates to be had concerning the value of covert observations. However, the role of the observer can vary in terms of the level of participation and degree of judgement. It is inevitable that the observer will act as a filter, meaning that there will be a degree of analysis prior to the recording of events. To a large extent observation is the 'natural' research method of teachers, as it so closely relates to their normal mode of operation in the classroom – particularly when the focus of the observation is the class or specific pupils within it. Perhaps the most important differences is the degree of focus and the structure of recording the observations (further details of observation for research can be found in Cohen *et al.*, 2000: ch. 17, and Moyles in Coleman and Briggs, 2002).

The analysis of documents within school can play a very important role in understanding how the school works. Policy documents are supposed to reflect practice and also be aspirational. They provide a means of comparing what is *actually* happening with what is *meant* to be happening in the school (particularly in respect of learning and teaching within subjects). Likewise, the mission statement offers a strong indication of the expected culture of the school. Minutes of meetings can be used to confirm decisions and the outcomes of discussions. Test results can be used to benchmark performance and for comparative purposes, both internally and externally. In all cases it is important to acknowledge the original purpose of the document, especially if this is different from the purpose your research is attempting to make of it.

Lomax (in Coleman and Briggs, 2002: 122) defines action research as 'trying out ideas in practice as a means of improvement and as a means of increasing knowledge'. It is very closely related to 'reflective practice' in many respects in that they are both based upon a self-reflective, self-critical approach to learning. Where action research goes beyond reflective practice is in its focus on the development of an enduring and potentially generizable knowledge base and in the extensive use of external (theoretical) input. It is, in many respects, the ideal way for a practitioner to make his or her first steps as a researcher with a focus on sustainable improvement.

Successful action research is a function of the values system within which you operate as both a teacher and a subject leader. It is, potentially, a very vulnerable approach, as it inevitably requires the researcher to push the envelope of his or her experience and expertise and expose him or herself to the critical review of others (their colleagues). It provides the perfect platform for the subject leader to initiate change within his or her own classroom to demonstrate the potential for improvement from which the rest of the school can learn.

It is likely that any one particular approach will only partially reveal the evidence that you are seeking and that you will need to apply a different approach, possibly with a different set of respondents to check the validity of your findings.

ASK YOURSELF

- How is my potential for performing research constrained?
- What practical options for research do I have?
- Which approach(es) will best reveal the evidence that I am searching for?
- How can I ensure that my findings are valid and reliable?

Analysing data and presenting recommendations to the SMT and staff

If the research and theoretical literature has been used as the basis for the design of your research tools, then it should be possible to compare your findings with those of others. It is important to focus back on the original questions or purposes that you set yourself to check that you have the evidence that you hoped for. Where your findings diverge from those the literature led you to expect then you, potentially, have a focus for action. Your evidence tells you are (educationally speaking) at position A, you want to be at B (according to your reading) so you now need to use the evidence and the literature to justify why B is so much better than A and what action is required to make the transition. Essentially this evidence, along with the analysis and action plan, is what needs to be presented to the senior management team within the school to inform the strategic decision-making processes. The recommendations, with action plan, are the end result of the research process; the rest provides the justification by adding weight to the argument.

There are many ways in which the analysis of evidence can be made more formal and, particularly in the case of quantitative data through the application of statistical tools, forceful. This is addressed very effectively in a range of specialist educational research texts, of which Cohen *et al.* (2000) is the most enduring and comprehensive for the practitioner-researcher.

- ◆ Do I have the evidence to support the recommendations that I am making?
- ◆ Have I explored all the potential options in taking my subject forward?
- ◆ How convinced am I of the validity of the decisions I am making?
- ◆ Is there additional research that I need to perform?

The relationship between research and evaluation

As outlined in Chapter 6, evaluation processes enable schools to analyse their accomplishments in a systematic way. If such evaluation is to be accurate, we need to measure the present position against original aims or targets so that we can gauge how far the individual or group has progressed. Logically, we may also wish to build in continual feedback about progress towards the achievement of these targets so that we have a continual loop of learning, feedback and evaluation that informs learning and teaching. MacBeath (1999) argues that the purposes of evaluation may be varied and that its objectives may include:

- organizational development;
- to improve teaching;
- to improve learning;
- political reasons;
- accountability; and
- professional development.

Thus Coleman (2005: 153) points out that evaluation as a concept may be neutral but in practice it can be used in many different ways, some of which challenge our conceptions about our own professionalism and the quality of the teaching that occurs within a school. For this reason evaluation may appear to be an objective process but in fact it may be value laden and reveal many insights about an organization. The things that we evaluate and the way that we evaluate them will betray much about what we hold to be important and worth while. We tend to evaluate items that are susceptible to quantifiable analysis such as examination or assessment successes or the effects on outcomes associated with curriculum innovations. This is partly because anything that produces quantifiable outcomes has an appeal to the evaluator in that it can be analysed with clarity, often using simple mathematical models. But we must remember that there are many things that cannot easily be measured in a quantifiable way such as developments in socialization skills and improvements in behaviour, attitude and motivation. We must then ask key questions such as: should we be attempting to evaluate the affective issues? Do we actually evaluate too much? We must remember that evaluation is not an end in itself; it is tool to assist us in making things better.

In essence evaluation is a form of applied research but this does not mean, of course, that it can only be carried out by professional researchers who have undergone research training (Coleman, 2005: 156). Having said that, it is true that some basic understanding of research techniques and terminology is useful in conducting evaluation. Traditionally this has been something of a neglected area in higher education generally in the UK but the notion of the research-informed practitioner, perhaps especially in education, has grown in recent years and this has led to a number of positive developments in teacher initial and in-service education.

MacBeath *et al.* (2000) characterize most evaluation methods as 'asking', which can be accomplished through:

- interviews;
- questionnaires;
- log or diary writing;
- observation and work shadowing; and
- focus group discussions.

The advantages, disadvantages and possible uses of these approaches are outlined in Table 12.1.

Table 12.1 Advantages, disadvantages and uses of different research and evaluation tools

Evaluation tool	Advantages	Disadvantages	Paradigm	Uses
Interviews	Allows in-depth responses	Notoriously time-consuming, transcription can be lengthy	Qualitative/ quantitative because interviews can pose both open and closed questions	Can gain detailed, sometimes sensitive and personal information from individuals

Table 12.1 Continued

Evaluation tool	Advantages	Disadvantages	Paradigm	Uses
Questionnaires	Can be distributed to large numbers of people and can collect large amounts of data swiftly	Can be expensive (such as postage), information may not be sufficiently detailed	Quantitative/qualitative because questions may ask for numeric or written answers	To obtain information on specific issues and prepare reports
Log or diary writing	Can elicit highly reflective and detailed accounts of situations and events	Can be difficult to negotiate because they can be time-consuming and sometimes difficult to write	Qualitative	To gain large amounts of high-quality data from individual teachers or school leaders
Observation and work shadowing	Can reveal behaviours and characteristics and group interactions that the subject/respondent may not themselves be aware of	Time-consuming and lengthy and subjective in interpretation	Largely qualitative but observation schedules can include carefully thought-out mapping techniques that are susceptible to quantitative analysis	Especially appropriate for examining teacher–pupil/pupil–pupil interactions in the classroom, playground or other social situations
Focus group discussions	May gain perspectives from a wide group of people very swiftly		Qualitative	Can be used to gain perspective from coherent groups (such as the SMT or departmental staff) or from diverse groups (such as staff in different departments or governors with varying responsi-bilities)

Evaluation thus crosses the boundaries between quantitative and qualitative methods and the main guiding principles on the methods employed should be ease of use and fitness for purpose. We must, however, bear in mind any subsumed ethical considerations when collecting data in the context of a school setting. Indeed it is incumbent on the evaluator to decide if the data collection is really required and, if so, the uses that it may be put to and how they may impact on the lives of pupils and their families and fellow practitioners in the future. We may collect data with clear and positive purposes in mind but we must be alert to the fact that such data may be employed by others for other means in the future, so access to data and data storage are also important issues. Some general issues that need to be addressed in research and evaluation include the following:

- What are the purposes of this research/evaluation?
- What is it seeking to measure and why?
- Have relevant permissions been sought (from senior staff such as the headteacher/from parents where relevant/from the pupils themselves where appropriate)?
- How will the data be analysed?
- How will the data be stored and who will have access to them?

Busher and Harris (2000: 24–5) suggest a three-stage process when evaluating change:

1 A pre-initiation stage when evaluative evidence has to be used to judge whether change or development is really needed and, if so, what type of change and development is most suitable and feasible.
2 An implementation stage where the evaluation process concentrates on providing evidence of the impact of change and highlights any difficulties incurred in the process.
3 An institutionalization phase when the purpose of evaluation is to make judgements of the overall impact of the change that has occurred.

The overarching principle behind such empirical analysis, whether it is styled as research or evaluation, should be to inform practice and to lead to reflective practitionership which improves the quality of the learning experiences of students.

The reflective middle leader

The concept of reflective teaching can be traced back to the work of John Dewey (1933), who contrasted routine action, defined by such factors as tradition, habit and authority, with reflective action, which involved a willingness to be involved in constant self-appraisal and development (Pollard, 2002: 12). Cenral to Dewey's argument was the notion that teachers needed to be open-minded and 'to have an active desire to listen to more sides than one, to give heed to facts from whatever sources they came, to give full attention to alternative possibilities' (1933: 29). Pollard (2002: 12–13) identifies seven key characteristics of reflective practice:

1 Reflective teaching implies an active concern with aims and consequences, as well as means and technical efficiency.
2 Reflective teaching is applied in a cyclical, spiralling process, in which teachers monitor, evaluate and revise their own practice continuously.
3 Reflective teaching requires competence in methods of evidence-based classroom inquiry, to support the progressive development of higher standards of teaching.
4 Reflective teaching requires attitudes of open-mindedness, responsibility and wholeheartedness.
5 Reflective teaching is based on teacher judgement, informed by evidence-based inquiry and insights from other research.
6 Reflective teaching, professional learning and personal fulfilment are enhanced through collaboration and dialogue with colleagues.
7 Reflective teaching enables teachers to mediate creatively in externally developed frameworks for teaching and learning.

This commitment to research-informed and reflexive practice is now firmly embedded in the national agenda. For instance, the TTA (2000) advises that effective teachers should:

● know how to find and interpret existing, high-quality evidence from a range of sources, such as research reports, other schools' experience of Ofsted inspection and performance data as a tool for raising standards;
● see professional development, which includes elements of research, as a means of improving classroom practice and raising standards, rather than an end in itself;
● see pedagogy as integral to learning; and
● interpret external evidence confidently, in relation to pupil or subject needs, rather than viewing it as a threat.

In essence we find ourselves in an unprecedented era of curriculum innovation linked to performance targets in our schools which has led to the emergence of an environment rich in performance data. It is more important than ever before that teachers elicit opportunities to evaluate their practice and that of their colleagues in co-operative ways in order to ensure that their professional role as reflective practitioners is both defended and enhanced.

Case study

Lesley has worked at Green Lane Lower School since qualifying to teach three years ago. She has already demonstrated a particular strength in her work with children with specific learning difficulties and has been attending enrichment training to improve her understanding of the needs of children who are on the autism spectrum. Her work alongside the special educational needs co-ordinator to support the training of teaching and support staff has been recognized by the senior management team and the school governors. She has been tasked with coaching two more-experienced members of the teaching staff who have autistic children in their classes. To ensure that her work has a lasting impact she has been reviewing research and theories derived from empirical studies to identify the most effective form her support of these teachers should take. For support, Lesley has enrolled on an MA course and is using this as a mean of evaluating the effectiveness of her coaching with a view to informing future practice at her school. She has recognized the importance and value of research as evidence on which to make informed decisions.

Summary

This chapter has provided a few basic approaches and tools to begin the process of ensuring that strategic decisions made by the school are founded in and justified by the outcomes of reliable evidence obtained through sound research methodology. All too often teachers fear that 'research' is something esoteric that can only be undertaken by university-based specialists. In fact teachers are expert observers, interviewers and analysts of the abundant data that are around them in their classrooms in the form of their daily interactions with pupils and other staff. Indeed, as this and earlier chapters have shown, there are very strong links between research and evaluation of the type that schools are used to undertaking as part of their reflective activities as professional teachers. Moreover, while this chapter has been aimed primarily at the practitioner purely working to improve the quality of learning and teaching within his or her school, it also provides a sound basis for research for academic purposes as part of undergraduate or postgraduate professional studies.

When conceptualizing this text the authors set themselves the aim of revealing the complex nexus of interconnections between professional practice, academic research and writing, national initiatives and public policy-making. We hope that this final chapter has provided an additional element in bridging and those all too frequently alienated realms.

References

Beacon Schools (2004) *Welcome to Beacon Schools* (online at http://www.standards.dfes.gov.uk/beaconschools/).

Brown, A. and Dowling, P. (1998) *Doing Research, Reading Research. A Mode of Interrogation for Education*. London: Falmer.

Bryman, A. and Burgess. R. (eds) (1994) *Analysing Qualitative Data*. London: Routledge.

Busher, H. and Harris, A. (2000) *Subject Leadership and School Improvement*. London: Paul Chapman Publishing.

Cohen, L., Manion, L. and Morrison, K. (2000) *Research Methods in Education* (5th edn). London: RoutledgeFalmer.

Coleman, M. (2005) 'Evaluation in education', in M. Coleman and P. Earley (eds) *Leadership and Management in Education: Cultures, Change and Context*. Oxford: Oxford University Press.

Coleman, M. and Briggs, A. (eds) (2002) *Research Methods in Educational Leadership and Management*. London: Paul Chapman Publishing.

Dewy, J. (1933) *How We Think*. Boston, MA: Heath.

DfEE (2001) *Continuing Professional Development*. London: HMSO.

Hammersley, M. (1995) *The Politics of Social Research*. London: Sage.

Joyce, B. (1991) 'The doors to school improvement', *Educational Leadership*, May: 59–62.

MacBeath, J. (1999) *Schools Must Speak for Themselves: The Case for School Self-evaluation*. London: Routledge.

MacBeath, J., Schratz, M., Meuret, D. and Jakbsen, L. (2000) *Self-evaluation in European Schools: A Story of Change*. London: Routledge.

Morrison, M. (2002) 'What do we mean by educational research', in M. Coleman and A. Briggs (eds) *Research Methods in Educational Leadership and Management*. London: Paul Chapman Publishing.

NCSL (2004) *Research and Development* (online at http://www.ncsl.org.uk/index.cfm?pageID=randd-index).

Pollard, A. (2002) *Reflective Teaching: Effective and Evidence-informed Professional Practice*. London: Continuum.

TTA (2000) *Improving Standards through Evidence-based Teaching*. London: TTA.

Recommended reading

Hopkins, D. (2002) *A Teacher's Guide to Classroom Research*. Milton Keynes: Open University Press.

Websites

AERA: American Education Research Association (http://www.aera.net/).
BERA: British Educational Research Association (http://bera.ac.uk).
CERUK: Current Educational Research in the UK (http://www.ceruk.ac.uk/ceruk/).
DfES Research-informed practice site (http://www.standards.dfes.gov.uk/research/).
ICSEI: International Congress for School Effectiveness and Improvement (http://www.edu.icsei/index.html).

Index

Added to a page number 'f' denotes a figure and 't' denotes a table.